FOUNDING VISION
FOR A FUTURE ARMY

Spiritual renewal and mission
in The Salvation Army

FOUNDING VISION FOR A FUTURE ARMY

Spiritual renewal and mission in The Salvation Army

by

Lieut-Colonel Alan Burns

United Kingdom Territorial Headquarters
101 Newington Causeway
London SE1 6BN

First published in 2012 by
Shield Books
© The Salvation Army
UK Territory Literary Unit
101 Newington Causeway
London SE1 6BN

ISBN 978-0-85412-857-0

Cover design by Jonathan Carmichael

SHIELD
BOOKS
© The Salvation Army
United Kingdom Territory with
the Republic of Ireland

Printed by UK Territory Print and Design Unit

With thanks to my ABC
(Alison, Becki and Cameron),
who supported me throughout the research
and writing of this book.

Abbreviations

ASV	*American Standard Version*
CEV	*Contemporary English Version*
KJV	*King James Version*
NIV	*New International Version*
SASB	*The Song Book of The Salvation Army*

Contents

Foreword

ONE of the signs of health in the life of any movement is that in every generation there will be a prophet or prophets who sound a convincing call to revisit the group's founding principles and regain its early focus. Alan Burns has managed to do this without harking back to a mythical rather than an actual past, and without prescribing a singular course of action as the only legitimate way of being The Salvation Army at this stage in our history.

Instead he takes us on a theological and sociological journey back to the remarkable spiritual giftedness of William Booth and the charismatic community that formed around this people's prophet. Booth's methods are less central to the author's thesis than the integrity of the primitive Christian Mission and Salvation Army as an authentic expression of the community that gathered around Jesus. The Salvationist understanding of Church is that together we are the gathered people of God radically indwelt – and often unpredictably empowered and directed in mission – by the Holy Spirit. As the author says, 'The Church does not exist to *do* God's mission in the world – the Church exists *as* God's mission in the world.'

Having our roots in the local corps (church) makes us a truly proletarian movement: that is, a movement 'of the people'. This manifests itself as a worshipping and serving body within the wider community. Although many people recognise us only for our work among the poor and socially marginalised, most of those who experience the Army do so through contact with local Salvationists who may be neighbours, friends or family – or just good people who can be relied upon in times of need.

Essentially, the local corps is an expression of what the Army is called to be in any given community, not just a functional unit doing what it is told by headquarters. In theological terms, if the corps is to be thought of as a branch of anything, it is a branch of the True Vine.

Salvationist readers and others will readily identify with the language used in this book. While the word 'charism' might be new to some, its application to teaching on soul-saving, holiness, serving and thinking prophetically will resonate with Army people across the world.

So also will Alan Burns's own quest to discover how his initial zeal for Christ and the gospel has weathered and seasoned over almost four decades of Christian leadership, as he reflects on how the God-given charisms of the primitive Salvation Army are expressed in Booth's Army today.

Ian Barr
Lieut-Colonel

Introduction

MY interest in mission stems from my introduction to The Salvation Army as an 18-year-old convert. When I made a commitment of my life to Christ in August 1972, my corps officer gave me a copy of the book *The General Next to God* by Richard Collier. This stimulating paperback tells the story of the Founder of The Salvation Army, William Booth. During those early days of my faith journey, this book was a key influence and a passion was lit in my heart to aspire to the vision of this godly and dynamic revivalist. I made a personal covenant that my priority in life would be to identify with what I now understand to be the mission of God – God the Evangelist, whose heart beats with a passion to reach the lost.

As a result of this, one of the first Salvation Army activities I embarked upon was selling *The War Cry* in the local pubs and bars. I confess my interest in the money raised was negligible, and remember being somewhat taken aback when given a collecting box. I wanted people to know Christ! I was also surprised that so few of us from the corps were engaging in this activity.

As well as evangelism, an accompanying desire as a new Christian was to reach up to God in prayer and to be a holy, authentic follower of Christ. My search for an experience of holiness took a while longer than I had hoped, but I remember the day when, as a cadet at The Salvation Army's training college, I realised Christ had sanctified my life and the joy this brought to my heart.

As I reflect on those early years of faith, I have come to realise there is a direct correlation between the intimacy of the relationship I was developing 'in Christ' and my earnest desire to be engaged in reaching the lost. The more I knew Christ personally the more he could be seen and known as I lived out my daily life. I found myself wanting to witness at my workplace, on the train and at every other opportunity I had.

This early 'epiphany' has required constant renewal as my journey through the last 37 years has taken many a twist and turn. My greatest fear as a young man was that of losing the zeal with passing time. A faith once on fire and focused can become disillusioned when circumstances, bitterness and regret begin to eat away at the roots of the missionary vision. Therefore, I've always believed that the Holy Spirit is able to renew me daily and to bring to completion that which was born in my heart in those early days (see Philippians 1:6). Paul's encouragement to Timothy to 'fan the flame' (see 2 Timothy 1:6 *NIV*) was not simply a spur to keep his relationship with Christ alive but a stimulus to stoke the passion for the mission of God in the world. I confess that I have not always 'fanned the flame' as I should have, but I thank God it hasn't gone out – that the Holy Spirit graciously, gently and consistently keeps this heart 'burning, burning' (*SASB* 206).

This book is born out of these two important themes – mission and spiritual renewal. In my experience they are inextricably linked. Without spiritual renewal, mission will atrophy and die over time. Without mission, spiritual renewal is a self-centred indulgence that will not impact our world or society.

We begin with a look at the origins of Salvation Army identity, which then leads us into a study of the charisms – gifts and graces endowed by the Holy Spirit – of the Founder and the founding Salvationists. Here we trace the work of the Holy Spirit in the birth story of the Army and trace the giftings that enabled it to engage in its God-ordained mission. Chapter Three focuses on the mission of God, reminding us that it is his, and that he invites us to partner with him. The next three chapters look at the dominant charisms of soul-saving, holiness and serving suffering humanity and how we can retrieve them through spiritual renewal. In the final chapter we reflect on the impact this will have on the modern-day Salvation Army, and prepare ourselves for what might happen as the Holy Spirit breathes his life into us. We consider the consequences of moving forward with God!

Although I offer some practical suggestions and observations, I am not prescribing solutions or driving the reader towards firm conclusions. My aim is to examine prevailing Salvation Army attitudes and paradigms in the early part of the 21st century. In some ways I am throwing a brick into a settled pond. However, my purpose is not to vandalise the Army, but to break through the viscosity of stale ideas that prevent the Holy Spirit from moving among us – and moving us forward.

I acknowledge that I write from a Western perspective. The demise of Christendom in the West is a given in my thinking. I make no distinction between Christianity as represented by the institutionalised Church and/or denomination and the world view presented by the Christian faith. Both are generally despised in the West. However, I am confident that, when people see the real thing in Christians, they will be compelled again to examine the new life offered in Christ.

I believe God has a purpose for The Salvation Army in this context, and that it lies in our roots – in what the Holy Spirit actually and unmistakeably did when he raised us up. Whatever God does with us in terms of spiritual renewal, we will always be connected to this purpose, so clearly articulated by General John Gowans: to save souls, grow saints and serve suffering humanity.

I pray that through this book God will allow me to make a small contribution towards The Salvation Army becoming again the effective, life-changing, transforming agent it was in the founding days Richard Collier wrote about all those years ago.

CHAPTER ONE

Identity Crisis

'Identity is the filter that every organism or system uses to make sense of the world. New information, new relationships, changing environments – all are interpreted through a sense of self... An organism will change to maintain its identity.' [1]

Margaret Wheatley

IDENTITY has become a major issue in recent years. In the United Kingdom the rise of identity theft is causing people to think carefully about the protection of their personal details.

While the identity of The Salvation Army may not actually have been 'stolen', it may be fair to say it is under threat. According to some, the Army in these early stages of the 21st century is experiencing an identity crisis.

If we were to eavesdrop on many a conversation between Salvationists, it would not take long to perceive that the discussion, which they summarise as 'putting the Army right', is in fact a conversation about the identity of the Movement.

It is not only the old chestnuts such as uniform-wearing and musical genre that feature in such talk, but also issues that concern mission and the way it is executed, such as the evangelistic effectiveness of both our social services and corps engagement with the community.

1

Some insist our Salvation Army identity lies in traditions, methodology and uniforms; others challenge us to think about what the 'essentials' or 'distinctives' are. Some people perceive our identity as fixed; others see it as fluid and flexible. For some the clue is in our ecclesiology (our way of 'doing church'), while others suggest that we lose our identity when we become too liturgical, or 'churchy'.

This book will explore the idea that the identity of The Salvation Army lies in the sovereign work of the Holy Spirit, particularly during the Movement's founding years. Specifically, the Holy Spirit gifted the founder/s with charisms that enabled them to accomplish the mission of God. As we will see, charisms are gifts and graces given by the Holy Spirit that result in measurable outcomes in the world. In looking at the 'gifts and graces' of soul-saving, holiness and serving suffering humanity, we can see how the Movement's identity and purpose began to take shape, and how the Army must be continually renewed in these charisms – by the Holy Spirit – as it pursues God's mission in every generation.

Identity and purpose
Purpose arises out of identity, which is why it is imperative to deal with the identity question thoroughly. The methods, traditions and behavioural habits that have developed in the Army over the years have become part of who we are. But inheriting and then regurgitating a methodology, without understanding its original purpose, is clearly not the smartest way of doing things.

I remember, as a young corps officer, my folk conducting open-air meetings at a virtually deserted bus station at 5.30 pm every Sunday. I learnt that 50 years ago it was the hub of the town's activity and therefore a great venue for this outreach. When I asked why this ineffective practice persisted, the answer was: 'Because we've always held our service here!' Who were we? In the perception of the Salvationists, we were faithfully evangelising, as Salvationists had always done in that place at that time. In the opinion of the (very few) bus travellers, we were a strange group of people making a strange noise at a strange time in a strange place.

Many believe that we have deviated somewhat from our original purposes. We sense that what we do now may need to be rethought, although we may not agree as to how that happens. What we can agree on is that our identity as Salvationists lies in the fact that we are first and foremost disciples of Jesus. The key question is: 'What kind of disciples are Salvationists?'

The supremacy of the local setting

There is a tension between the identity of the national organisation that is The Salvation Army and the identity of a local Salvation Army setting. It is true that the local setting benefits enormously from its identification with an international body of more than a million Salvationists in more than 120 countries. However, a local corps or centre also needs to establish its own identity as a fellowship and retain a sense of autonomy, ownership and responsibility over its mission and witness in the community it serves.

It is vital to remember that The Salvation Army's true identity lies in local settings. This is not always apparent, neither is it necessarily understood or accepted. However, it needs to be emphasised, not simply because these places are the delivery points of Army mission but because there is a theological basis for this assertion. In the 1900s, Roland Allen, an Anglican missionary to North China from 1895 to 1903, wrote an excellent little book called *Missionary Methods, St Paul's or Ours*. In it, he alerted readers to the differences between the missionary methods of St Paul and those the modern Church adopts. Allen observed that St Paul founded churches as autonomous units and complete entities that were not in any way dependent on institutional benevolence and patronage:

'So far as the foundation of the churches is concerned, the writer of Acts intends to represent St Paul's work as complete. The churches were really established. Whatever disasters

3

fell upon them in later years, whatever failure there was, whatever ruin, that failure was not due to any insufficiency or lack of care and completeness in the Apostle's teaching or organisation. When he left them he left them because his work was fully accomplished.'[2]

So, for example, when Paul founded the church in Thessalonica, the established church at Antioch (the 'mother' church) was not permitted to have any authority over this fledgling church plant. Paul trusted God and the people of Thessalonica to develop the church in that place. He resourced it so it could develop autonomously when he left five months after founding it.

According to Paul's methodology of establishing and planting churches, the local church should be a self-governing, self-financing, self-propagating body. Paul did not create a culture of dependency, but of completion. All the churches he founded in a relatively short space of time became complete, autonomous units – even though they were not, of course, perfect. In fact, the concept of churches as denominational institutions actually arose out of the success of local churches. The first Pope started out as the pastor of the local church in Rome.

So it is the local church and not the institution that gives the Church its identity. Organisation and structure follow revival; they seldom precede or instigate it. In his book *Transforming Mission*, theologian David Bosch asserts that:

> 'The church is the church because of what happens in local churches' *martyria, leitourgia, koinonia* and *diakonia*… the church is an event among the people rather than an authority addressing them, or an institution possessed of elements of salvation, of doctrines, and offices…'[3]

From Salvation Army history, it can be argued that the rapid proliferation of local corps/centres, which by 1900 numbered more than 1,000 in the UK alone, subsequently turned The Salvation Army into an institution with an elaborate centralised structure of divisions and national chains of command. Yet the key to the Movement's mission and identity was not in those structures, it was in the local corps/centres.

Of course, there is value to mission in a healthy relationship between local churches and the wider denomination. For one thing, it brings the issue of accountability into the picture. Another significant benefit is a sense of mutual mission with other corps/centres and the facilitation of resource-sharing through regional and national organisational structures and networks. However, it remains that *the local church is the primary agent of mission.*

When I was a young officer the culture was, unfortunately, one of paternalism, where officers from headquarters would 'inspect and monitor' my ministry and mission. I was usually left to feel that I was missing the mark in terms of their institutional expectations. The impression given was that the 'important' part of the Army was not at the coalface of mission endeavour, but in the structures to which they belonged.

I am pleased to say this situation has greatly improved. In our current climate, 'headquarters' has been encouraged to think more in terms of resourcing and supporting local corps/centres, although frustrating remnants do remain. It is still a work in progress.

Traditional conservatives

In terms of Salvation Army identity, it may be useful to recognise two broad categories of people who represent either end of a continuum: traditional conservatives and radical (lower case) liberals.

The more traditional conservative Salvationist asserts that adherence to inherited traditions demonstrates true Salvationism and faithfulness to God, who raised us up and inspired our founders – by whom I mean the Booth family and other early-day pioneers. Therefore, the preservation of tradition is paramount to the future success of the mission of The Salvation Army. In so doing there are things they will relentlessly defend, such as the music used in our worship. For them, the Salvation Army songbook, brass bands and songster brigades are integral to our identity.

Other 'essentials' for traditional conservatives would include uniform-wearing, regulations governing membership of sections and a person's commitment to these groups. Decline is attributed to a lack of commitment on the part of (mainly) young people who will simply not do the things they themselves did when they were young.

The 'inherited Army' is the Army they grew up with, and there is room for no other. Their own corps reflects and promotes these values and practices, and they find themselves struggling to understand why anyone would want to introduce anything new.

These traditional Salvationists are often, though by no means always, at least third-generation Salvationists. Their arguments are not totally without merit. The Army's reputation relies on visibility, and the reinforcement in the public arena of these functions may be necessary in order for our identity to survive. Indeed, there is an argument developing for more open-air meetings and a greater uniformed presence in high streets and shopping centres. Effectively, the rationale promoted is that we need to reinforce the old methods with greater passion. British author Eddie Gibbs, in his book *Followed or Pushed*, describes such behaviour perfectly: 'They are unrelenting when challenged with being out of step with the times, because, in their opinion, it is everyone else who has changed step, not they.'[4]

The difficulty with this stance is not that it brings a historical perspective to the challenge of decline, but that it does not go back far enough in The Salvation Army's history. Traditional conservatives see the immediate past – the traditions they learnt in their lifetime – but not the distant founding days where people were probably more radical than the group they fear at the opposite end of the continuum! As theologian and futurist Leonard Sweet observes in *Soul Tsunami*: 'The problem with the church today is not that it is "too traditional"; the problem with the church today is that it is not traditional enough. It has held the future to a frozen version of the past.'[5]

Radical liberals

At the other extreme, radical liberal Salvationists hold the values mentioned above lightly, even sometimes with disdain. This group wants to redesign the Army for a 21st-century audience whose world view is postmodern and future-orientated. They argue that The Salvation Army as described by conservative Salvationists belongs to a now defunct 'Christendom era' and has little or no relevance for the early 21st century.

To their way of thinking, the Army needs to reposition, reinvent and rebrand itself; in order to do this it must let go of any tradition that they believe will hold it back: brass bands, uniform-wearing, outmoded forms of music, misplaced commitment to no longer relevant activities – all must be done away with[6]. The Army of today must shed itself of non-essentials and rediscover its identity with new vision and new openness to God.

They argue that in the early days, when there was no historical context, there was little reference to precedent or accepted modes of operation, and in this respect often quote William Booth and other Army pioneers. They recognise and describe a generation that rejects and distrusts institutional religion and therefore cannot be reached for Christ through it. For the liberal Salvationist the more informal, relevant and accessible the Army becomes, the more it will regain its identity and purpose – even its mission.

Without wishing to stereotype it into the definition articulated above, ALOVE – which resources the faith journey of Salvation Army young people through four 'essentials' of faith: worship, discipleship, mission and social action – is an excellent illustration of a generation of young people trying to rebrand the Army and to position it to reach their peers. Indeed, after a great deal of

7

deliberation over a title for this new expression of The Salvation Army, the founders of ALOVE came up with 'The Salvation Army – for a New Generation'. If we accept that the name of a new movement holds clues to its identity, then this title and its strapline reveal two astonishing facts: this new expression wanted to identify with The Salvation Army and it wanted to rebirth the Founder's dream and mission in a new generation. The correlation of ALOVE's Mission Statement to the Founder's dream is amazing[7]. How ALOVE actually works out that vision in practice, however, continues to divide opinion.

Tensions

It is important to refer to the often unhealthy tension between those at either end of the identity spectrum. It lurks beneath the surface in many settings and has the capacity to cause divisions and thwart the mission. Liberal Salvationists may view the conservatives with distrust and even dislike. They have been heard to refer to conservative Salvationists as lacking in spiritual depth, as never having understood the call to discipleship, as being outward in their show of religion, as being stuck in a time warp, and so on. On the other hand, the conservatives can unhelpfully describe their 'nemesis' as unreliable, unwilling to deliver anything of substance, lacking in commitment and even as being troublemakers intent on the destruction of the Army's heritage.

Both the traditional conservatives and radical liberals fear loss as they consider the inevitability of change and face an uncertain future. The traditionalists may fear losing their established methods and style of doing things. People in the liberal group may fear a loss of flexibility and openness to the wind of the Spirit. The question being asked by both groups is: 'What will I lose by conceding ground?'

The answer is not easy, but our identity will not be recovered merely by changing *what we do* – the things we let go of or hold on to; we also need to consider *who we are*.

When God called Moses to lead the people out of Egypt into the Promised Land, Moses' question was one of identity: 'Who are you?' he asked God at the burning bush. God told Moses it was enough for him to know that: 'I am who I am' (Exodus 3:14). William Booth's actions stemmed from his vision of what God intended The Salvation Army to be. Vision is crucial to identity. Where it doesn't exist, the people perish (Proverbs 29:18 *KJV*) – or as one commentator says, the people don't hang around!

Birth – the secret of identity
Let me say again: purpose arises out of identity. We do what we do because of who we are. Caesarea Philippi was a turning point in the ministry of Jesus. He purposefully set his face towards Jerusalem after a conversation with his disciples which hinged on the question of his identity. '"What about you?" [Jesus] asked them. "Who do you say I am?" Peter answered, "You are the Messiah"' (Mark 8:29).

Who are we? Get this right, and everything else will follow.

I believe The Salvation Army has done a great deal of work in recent years on the purpose question: 'What are we here for?' – and paid too little attention to the identity question: 'Who are we?'

The Alban Institute's Alice Mann suggests the identity question is best answered by returning to our birth story and exploring the information surrounding that event. She writes: 'These earliest moments in a congregation's story contain powerful bits of genetic information that will express themselves in the rest of the life cycle.'[8]

Mann is not alone in this assertion. Robert Dale makes the same suggestion in his book *To Dream Again,* but goes on to say that identity lies in the founder's vision and dream. And Howard Snyder, in his excellent book *Decoding the Church,* suggests we look at the DNA of the church, present at the birth of that church, in order to discover the secrets of spiritual renewal.

Hence, The Salvation Army's identity question is best answered by visiting the early founding stories and founding vision. The identity of The Salvation Army is God-given, and I contend that the

9

answers to our current identity crisis lie in our birth story. In the following chapters we will explore this concept, reflecting on the work of the Holy Spirit among the founders of the Army as he gifted them to fulfil God's mission in the world.

It is in the charisms of the founders that we find the clues to our identity. As we discover them, may we detect the breath of the Spirit calling us to renewal.

CHAPTER TWO

The Charisms of the Founders

WHEN God raised up The Salvation Army the Holy Spirit accomplished something extraordinary in terms of the mission of God in the world.

There are many elements of the founders' story which can only be attributed to the unique and deliberate work of the Holy Spirit. In describing these divine initiatives the word 'charism' is an appropriate depiction. This word will be recognised, in part, from the word 'charismatic' which can describe qualities of leadership. It is also used in reference to the phenomenon of the 'charismatic movement'.

Put simply, the theological word 'charism' describes a gift or grace of the Holy Spirit that results in quantifiable, measurable outcomes resulting from action in the world.

The advantage of this lesser-used 'charism' is that it takes the focus away from human effort and ingenuity and attributes the giftings found in an individual, or group, to the Holy Spirit. While others have written about the 'essentials' and 'distinctives' of Salvation Army identity, these two expressions may not adequately describe the Holy Spirit's activity and intention in raising up The Salvation Army. 'Charism' conveys a more precise definition of the activity of God in the lives of the founders and, therefore – in the attributing of credit for the Movement's origin – the glory belongs to God.

What then is a charism? To answer this question fully, we will look at three areas in which charisms feature.

Charisms and theology

In Roman Catholic theology, and in particular the spiritual renewal of religious life outlined in the directives of Vatican II, the word charism is used to describe the gifts and graces of the Holy Spirit in the life of the founder and the founding members of an organisation. The term *char* is translated: 'To condescend, to grant grace, to give, to lavish.' Nouns ending with the suffix –*ma* suggest resulting action; the Greek word *charisma* could therefore be described as 'a concrete outcome of the grace given'[1].

Note the subtle distinction between charisms and spiritual gifts. The latter, such as preaching, teaching and administration, are gifts that the Holy Spirit gives to an individual, both to help him or her grow in grace and to contribute to the body of Christ. Charisms, on the other hand, refer particularly to those gifts that benefit others (outside the Church) and result in transformation in the world. American Professor of Theology Doris Donnelly says: 'Charism is both a call and an empowerment to do ministry [to others] in and beyond the Church.'[2]

The word *charism* appears 17 times in the New Testament, mainly in the writings of Paul and chiefly in Romans, Timothy and Corinthians. Peter also uses this word in his first letter (1 Peter 4:10).

The term is often used in Roman Catholic writings in reference to the origins of holy communities and orders. For example, the founder of a new order of nuns or monks would be required to convince the Church, by satisfying certain criteria, that the founding came about as a result of a charism or charisms in his or her life, or in the lives of the founding members[3]. For this tradition, a fundamental requirement of the charism of the founder is that the new order intends to remain within the boundaries of the broader Roman Catholic Church. The Church is then able to affirm the new order's unique contribution and gifting to the whole Church, and indeed the world. This allows the order, as it uses those charisms, to remain autonomous as it makes its distinct contribution to the mission of God and yet to retain its place within the Church.

Another requirement of charisms is that there is always a parallel to be drawn between the founder and their followers and Jesus and his disciples. It could be argued, then, that the charism goes back not only to the birth of that community, but to the origins of Christianity, to Jesus and his disciples in Galilee.

This latter requirement is a useful benchmark, or test, for recognising charisms. If the Church is commissioned to continue to bring to fruition the redemptive purposes of Christ in the world, it is logical to assume that, as the body of Christ, a community will continue to fulfil all aspects of Christ's purpose in terms of its identity and mission. If the community disconnects itself from its founding story, one may expect the charisms to dry up and its effectiveness to diminish.

So, is it possible to trace the charisms in the story of The Salvation Army's Founder – William Booth – and his early followers back to the life of Jesus and his disciples? If it is, then we need also to ask how successive generations have fared in their response to this: how the founding charisms influenced different motifs (patterns of thought) in subsequent generations. In the handing down of these charisms, has loyalty to and passion for them been sustained – or has it decreased?

Connections between the charisms and Christ's sacrifice on the cross will always manifest themselves. A founder can sometimes be a disturbing person who challenges the status quo. There is always a cost connected with following the founder's path. This is because they are at the pioneering edge of the Church and will call the Church to ministry and mission outside its established parameters. The distinctive of a charism is marked by a person's willingness, like Christ, to sacrifice themselves for the benefit of others.

There is also a sense of resurrection which, for the disciples, had its outworking at Pentecost, when the Holy Spirit filled them with fire. Donnelly points out that the disciples' resurrection actually occurred at Pentecost:

> '[Jesus'] execution by the state shocked and terrorised his followers (the disciples) just as it was meant to. His resurrection also shocked them. But it did not revive them. They were still cross shocked, so numbed by his death that they could hardly believe the life before their eyes. Pentecost marks the disciples' resurrection, a resurrection by fire.'[4]

The Holy Spirit fired the disciples into life and gifted them for mission. It is no wonder that William Booth's prayer 'Thou Christ of burning, cleansing flame, send the fire!' (*SASB* 203), is also sung in this modern era in other denominations, as a new tune has brought it to the attention of a new generation of believers.

Charisms and sociology

There is also a sociological foundation to charisms. German philosopher and sociologist Max Weber, one of the principal architects of modern social science, identifies a long list of qualities relating to a person with charismatic authority, with the key elements relating to William Booth being:

- *Recognition of the leader's mission by the followers.* The followers follow, not merely because the leader is elected or positioned formally but because they recognise and own the leader's mission.

- *A need to stand outside the ties of the present order of things.* The charismatic leader lives and works at a distance from the world. Office-bearing, money and other vestiges of power are not of primary interest to this leader. Weber quotes the Jesuits, who vow not to become part of the Church hierarchy and who decline to hold office

14

by choosing instead to stand outside the bureaucratic structure. We can think here of William Booth's relationship to the Methodist Church, in which he did not seek career advancement.

- *Credibility comes from within.* It is through the outcomes, resulting from the charisms, that the leader proves his or her worthiness to engage others. There is an accepted recognition of a divine imperative to the charismatic leader's mission. The ability to lead is derived from a gift, a grace bestowed on such a figure – an almost mystical quality that defies precise definition and which cannot be gained through formal processes such as training and education.

Weber also describes the charismatic leader, in religious circles, as a prophet. This is because a prophet is equipped to bring a divine command that causes a break with tradition or custom. He cites Jesus as a charismatic leader because of his ability to break with the traditions of the day. The charismatic leader is seen as something of a revolutionary. Therefore, according to Weber, the charism of the founder – the prophet – is crucial to the development of a movement. Any genuine charismatic authority figure, he suggests, must make his or her own the words: 'It is written ... but I say unto you.'[5]

Weber sees charisms as unusual, spontaneous and creative. They are unusual in that they are not found in any other person at that time. They are spontaneous in that they contradict predictable norms and routines. They are creative in that a new movement is born and new forms of being emerge. Weber's conclusions would lead us to suggest that charisms are given in order that something may be achieved in the world which could not be ordinarily accomplished without them.

If we develop this thought, we could argue that William Booth and the early Salvationists were gifted to deliver the mission of

God in a new way – in a way that the Church Universal at the time was unable to do. Of course, the charisms did not actually disconnect Booth from the true body of Christ – the universal, catholic, Christian Church – but he clearly could not accomplish his God-given mission by staying within Methodism.

Charisms and ecclesiology

In writing about the ecclesiology of charisms, Donnelly affirms that charisms are by their very nature unpredictable and, when introduced into an institution such as the Church, could be a recipe for chaos. Yet, she says:

> 'There is something predictably institutional about the Church within which the Spirit works through the charisms of its members. The charisms functioning independently of the structures would be chaos, while the institution without the charisms would be monotonous, uniform and lifeless. So each needs the other.'[6]

This reminds us that without constant reference to and exercise of charisms, our Movement could easily atrophy in terms of spiritual life and warfare.

We need to be constantly reminded that structure, policy and regulation ought never to overshadow the charisms. Jesus spoke about the Holy Spirit being like the wind blowing 'wherever it wishes' (John 3:8) and we need charisms to work in our structures in ways that we might not be able to predict but which are Holy Spirit-led. During an organisation's life cycle there will be periods when charisms rise to the surface and govern direction. Then there are other times when issues of structure and policy are prone to hold sway and the charisms can get lost. American professor of Church and Ministry Martin Saarinen wrote about this, pointing frequently to corrective factors in the life cycle that produce rebirth and health in the Church. He says a healthy congregation is one 'that has learned creative use of the inherent conflicts between the visionary and the pragmatic, the emotional and the rational. It is characterised by a redemptive and creative oscillation between people and programme concerns, with a strong sense of mission as the fulcrum.'[7]

While Saarinen does not use the language of charisms he implicitly acknowledges the tensions we have been considering. Thankfully, he affirms that decline and death are not inevitable if leaders and congregations open themselves to the wind of God's Spirit. Depending on which voice the congregation listens to at crisis points in its development, he says, it will either grow or decline/die. It is the congregation's and its leader's responsibility to select the way to respond, he asserts.

Charisms and William Booth

William Booth was a founder who received gifts from the Holy Spirit that were clearly evident in his life and ministry. These charisms uniquely equipped him at a particular time in history to accomplish, as a partner in the mission of God, what could not be achieved if The Salvation Army were not present in the world. Even those who were not his followers saw Booth as an extraordinary person. Much was written about him in the newspaper editorials of his day and many biographies have been written in the years since his death. A former deputy leader of the Labour Party, Roy Hattersley, author of one of the more recent accounts, referred to William and Catherine Booth when he wrote: 'As saints, they were at best, second rate. As human beings they were remarkable by any standards – heroic, confident, indomitable, and full of hope and love for each other and their fellow men.'[8]

The charisms are not private property and their end is not personal gratification or blessing. The end of the charism is the building up of other people – as Donnelly says, they are 'unique gifts for the common good'[9]. This definition is another benchmark for any claim to charisms we identify in The Salvation Army, William Booth and his founding followers.

The charisms we will identify in the following chapters and attribute as belonging to The Salvation Army will be tested against the two specific definitions we have considered: the parallel between the founder and their followers with Jesus and his disciples; and the building up of others, particularly those outside the church.

ROOTS

Before we move on, let us look briefly at some compelling evidence that spiritual renewal, rooted in the charisms, is already under way in The Salvation Army.

Very few people would argue that, within the UK, the most significant renewal movement within the Army in the past 20 years has been the ROOTS movement. At its peak, almost 5,000 delegates attended the annual weekend conference, which was unashamedly about spiritual renewal and mission.

ROOTS started its life in 1994 when a small group of young Salvationists, led by Phil Wall, retreated to a venue in South Wales for a weekend. It was advertised as a time of mission and renewal. It caught the interest and attention of about 400 people who signed up to share this time together. Two aspects of the ROOTS phenomenon are relevant to this study of charisms.

The first is the name. In a desire to capture the essence of renewal and the future, the young pioneers of ROOTS went backwards – back to the roots, or birth story, of The Salvation Army. What were they looking for there? I suggest they were – and still are – subconsciously looking for the charisms of the founders.

Secondly, this search led the founding group to develop a vision statement for the movement, outlining core values for renewal and mission in The Salvation Army in the UK, such as a passion for the lost, a pragmatic determination to communicate the gospel in appropriate and culturally relevant ways, and embracing a sacrificial and dedicated lifestyle as an act of devotion to God and the world. In the full list, the first four core values relate to the charism of soul-saving – the conversion of sinners. The fourth and fifth relate to the charism of serving suffering humanity, while the final four relate to the charism of holiness of life[10].

The ROOTS statement's correlation to the charisms is hugely significant. A new generation of young – and some not so young – Salvationists seems to have commenced a 'new curve', one which, it appears, God is blessing by bringing spiritual renewal to scores of people. Most importantly, this renewal retains a vital connection to the charisms of the founders.

What ROOTS has succeeded in demonstrating is how to rework the charisms in a new generation. This new generation has remained strongly connected to The Salvation Army but has attempted to reinvent it, capturing the imagination of our youth. They feel part of something new, yet still connected to what has happened historically. Interestingly, analysis shows that ROOTS is widely supported by all generations.

To sum up, I quote Doris Donnelly again, who says: 'At the risk of oversimplifying, charisms are a very special variety of gifts dispensed through the Holy Spirit in the Church and the world, as needed, for the common good.'[11]

Where we find lists of charisms in the New Testament they are not exhaustive, nor are they intended to be rigidly descriptive. Indeed, the very term charism defies precise 'scientific' description as it is by definition an activity of our sovereign God.

However, the charisms may be summarised thus:

- A special variety of gifts of the Holy Spirit, freely and lavishly given to individuals in every era of church life.

- Gifts given which are not for private use or aggrandisement, but given to empower an individual, or individuals, to do ministry in and beyond the Church.

- Gifts given to the founder and founding members which facilitate the missionary purposes of God to be fulfilled in any era by the new order or institution in a unique way.

The charisms are distinctly the property of the Holy Spirit, and their outworking in the world towards others in need is the validation of them. 'A tree is known by the kind of fruit it bears' (Matthew 12:33).

CHAPTER THREE

The Mission of God

INSPIRED by the motto created by General John Gowans, the Mission Statement of the United Kingdom Territory with the Republic of Ireland reads: 'Called to be disciples of Jesus Christ, The Salvation Army United Kingdom Territory with the Republic of Ireland exists to save souls, grow saints, and serve suffering humanity.' As we have seen in reference to ROOTS, this statement also captures the charisms.

Do these two initiatives provide evidence that the Holy Spirit calls us to renewal? I think so.

In the late 1980s and early 1990s there was an intentional focus on mission statements in The Salvation Army in the UK. In light of this, almost every corps and centre in Britain, including Territorial Headquarters, created a mission statement, and in doing so considered again the primary purpose for which they existed. For many it was an exciting process and brought signs of spiritual renewal as connections were made to their core purposes.

Some of the very early attempts read more like a book and were impossible to recall. The statements were often printed and framed and sometimes placed in foyers or other prominent places in our buildings. However, the importance of these statements has diminished somewhat over time. People have forgotten them, or misunderstood what mission statements were intended to be and to whom they actually belonged.

I realised this many years ago. In one of our first corps, my wife and I worked with the leadership team to create a mission statement. It was a struggle that lasted several weeks. One evening one of our members, Joe, said something profound. He pointed out that we are not required to 'invent' a mission statement, explaining that Jesus had already told us what to do and that his instructions to his followers were simple. Joe said the essential outline for any mission statement could be discovered in the Great Commission and the Great Commandment: make disciples of all nations and love each other. He suggested we keep it simple and just do what Jesus told us to do. Within no time we had created our mission statement based on these imperatives from Christ.

Over the years I have come to realise how truly profound that insight was. What Joe had identified for me was that the mission statement we were trying to create was already in existence and that it belonged to the Creator God himself. To have imagined that we could invite God to partner us in *our* mission was arrogant and completely back-to-front thinking. What Joe said shifted the emphasis to where it really belonged – to God. It dawned on us that it is *his* mission and he has invited us, and in fact created the Church to be, his partner in his mission.

We realised we had to ask what kind of corps we needed to become in order to join God in his mission in the world.

A theology of mission

According to David Bosch, it was theologian Karl Barth who first articulated a theology of mission as the activity of God. His work led to an understanding that mission was not primarily the activity of the Church, but that mission is the nature and passion of God himself. God is a missionary God and he birthed the Church to be an agent of that mission. Paul says in 1 Corinthians 3:9: 'For we are partners working together for God.' This is an awesome privilege.

In order to gain a clear understanding of mission we have to explore the theological foundations in Scripture. When referring to mission, the Roman Catholic Church uses the term Missio Dei – the mission of God. The term is used to describe how the Father, Son and Holy Spirit relate to one another. It describes, within the Trinity, a relationship of movement as the Father sends the Son and the Son sends the Spirit: 'Jesus said to [the disciples] again, "Peace be with you. As the Father sent me, so I send you." Then he breathed on them and said, "Receive the Holy Spirit"' (John 20:21-22).

What Missio Dei does, in fact, is to describe what God is like. It affirms that God is a *sending* God and that he is a *sent* God. When any of us encounter God, we do so in Jesus Christ, who has been sent to save us. This redemption activity is the essence of God's mission. As I recall The Salvation Army's founding story and hear of William Booth's passion for soul-saving and holiness, I find a correlation with Jesus commissioning his disciples and sending them, telling them to 'go':

> 'Jesus drew near and said to them, "I have been given all authority in heaven and on earth. Go, then, to all peoples everywhere and make them my disciples: baptise them in the name of the Father, the Son, and the Holy Spirit, and teach them to obey everything I have commanded you. And I will be with you always, to the end of the age"' (Matthew 28:18-20).

A missionary Salvation Army is an Army that has been sent.

Mission in the Old Testament
While there may be those who think that mission is absent from the Old Testament, Bosch points out in his book *Transforming Mission* that the Old Testament is vital to our understanding of mission[1]. Israel was created by God as a nation, he says, having been rescued and redeemed by God, who led the nation out of Egypt as a witness to all the nations. Therefore Israel and its history represent the arena and context for the missionary activity of God who wanted, through his chosen people, to reach the whole world with his salvation.

The basis of his relationship with Israel was his covenant made at Mount Sinai. Through a number of key individuals the activity of God can be seen in the nation's history. He is the God of Abraham, Jacob, Isaac, Moses – and these men are evidence of his work in Israel's past. The story of Abraham illustrates the missionary nature of God, whose heart beats on behalf of all who perish:

> 'I make this covenant with you: I promise that you will be the ancestor of many nations. Your name will no longer be Abram, but Abraham, because I am making you the ancestor of many nations. I will give you many descendants, and some of them will be kings. You will have so many descendants that they will become nations' (Genesis 17:4-6).

Christopher Wright, of Langham Partnership International, points out in his book *The Mission of God* that the context for the promises given to Abraham was set against the backdrop of the wickedness and sin of Sodom and Gomorrah. He invites us to note especially the contrast between a holy calling and promise and the degenerate, sinful, lost cities. He suggests that Sodom could represent the 21st-century world:

> 'It is clear that Sodom was used as a paradigm – a model of human society at its worst and of the inevitable and comprehensive judgment of God on such wickedness. It was a place filled with oppression, cruelty, violence, perverted sexuality, idolatry, pride, greedy consumption and void of compassion and care for the needy.'[2]

Remarkably, it is into this context that the missionary God called Abraham. Is it not true that any place filled with oppression, cruelty, violence, perverted sexuality, idolatry, pride and greedy consumption is a mission field? Any place void of compassion and care for the needy provides the context of God's mission.

Abraham was called into a godless arena, yet the trigger for God's action in Sodom was not the appalling sin of the people there – but the cries of the victims of those sins, those who suffered as a result of injustice and oppression.

In the Old Testament, Sodom stood for a world under judgment. Abraham was not called out of the land of Haran to some comfortable lifestyle but to Sodom and Gomorrah, because God had a missionary purpose for him – to save his children.

Abraham was the key to God's whole missionary purpose for history – for humanity. This is why Abraham's story is so important to a good biblical theology of the mission of God.

How Abraham responded is also a key ingredient. He turned to intercession (Genesis 18:23-32). In these verses we read the story of the conversation between Abraham and God as they appeared to be bargaining for souls. Abraham found God immensely accommodating.

The initial bid from Abraham – 50 righteous people – was met by successive reductions, which were willingly accepted by God. God was clearly far more merciful than Abraham had hoped. Judgment fell not because 50 could not be found, but because there were not even 10 – not even one.

However, Abraham's intercession did not fail. He asked that God would spare the righteous and not sweep them away with the wicked (18:23). Lot and his daughters were rescued, as were the surrounding villages which had been suppressed by these cities. Abraham assumed the role of an intercessor. He prayed for these wicked cities – even though they were beyond redemption. Intercessory prayer has missional significance.

Wright helpfully points out that Abraham's call to leave Haran in Genesis 12 was coloured with the idea that, in choosing Israel from the nations, God did not do so because it was different from the 70 or so other nations (Genesis 10) that existed at the time. All the nations, including Israel, had refused to listen to God and respond to him. The choice of Israel was not made to exclude the others. In fact, the opposite is true – it was to be through Israel that the nations of the world were to be blessed and find God's favour. Israel was chosen for the mission of God.

William Booth and his followers were also moved by injustice and oppression. What is the motivation behind the missionary heartbeat of God? It is his love and care, his compassion – his righteousness and justice. It is the suffering of the oppressed that breaks God's heart. The way of the Lord, the way of holiness, is to bring righteousness and justice for the oppressed, and to stand against the oppressor.

As we journey back to our founding story, we observe the culture and context into which God spoke to William Booth, that of 19th-century Britain. Booth was based in London and we know it was the sight of the godless, lost masses that moved him in his spirit. He saw, as God saw, people who were lost and in need of a Saviour.

I believe this has much to say to the 21st-century Salvation Army. We are living in an increasingly pagan and godless society. The description of Sodom certainly resonated with conditions in 19th-century Britain – in their intensity if not in the scale of the social climate. Much more aligned to godless and spiritually bankrupt Sodom is our spiritual plight as a nation in the 21st century. Is God speaking to the Army and calling us to mission and renewal?

General John Larsson thought so. In his first article written to Salvation Army officers following his election in 2002 he wrote that he believed The Salvation Army 'is going through a time of the most remarkable process of renewal'. He went on to say: 'And if in this process of renewal, we as an Army succeed in recapturing our passion for mission and develop a new self-understanding of the unique contribution we are meant to make, even greater things await the Army in the future.'[3]

Other great events in the Old Testament point us in the direction of God's mission. The Exodus reminds us of the struggle of a nation for freedom from bondage. The Book of Jonah contains another interesting missionary insight. Is it about a reluctant prophet or a gracious God? Jonah certainly responded to God's calling and sending – but by going in the opposite direction. Ironically, Jonah the evangelist slept while the pagan sailors prayed. The people of Nineveh heard and repented while Jonah moaned and complained. While the people repented, Jonah did not. He complained that God was too generous and merciful, and was unhappy and angry about what God had done:

> 'So he prayed, "Lord, didn't I say before I left home that this is just what you would do? That's why I did my best to run away to Spain! I knew that you are a loving and merciful God, always patient, always kind, and always ready to change your mind and not punish. Now, Lord, let me die. I am better off dead than alive." The Lord answered, "What right do you have to be angry?"' (Jonah 4:2-4).

Former Tutor in Mission at St John's College in Nottingham, Roger Bowen's conclusions to the story of Jonah challenge our commitment to God's mission:

1. God is more missionary than we are.

2. We are often afraid of mission and do not want to evangelise.

3. We often misunderstand and misrepresent our God.

4. True love for God can often be found outside the Church.

5. It is often hard for us to see what is happening when God works in new ways.

6. Mission does not make us successful, it makes us amazed and humble.[4]

The call to mission reminds us that we have a responsibility to see ourselves as 'sent'. We must behave like the God we follow: self-emptying, self-surrendering, committed to reaching others, caring for the poor and marginalised. All of this is evident in Jesus – and the primary characteristic of the Christian is to be like Christ.

The Church as God's mission
The Church does not exist to *do* God's mission in the world – the Church exists *as* God's mission in the world. As the Church accepts the mission of God that sends it into the world it most truly reflects the nature and life of God himself. The thinking behind 'being sent' has some significant implications for us. For example, where does mission take place?

If we belong to a church where the theology is 'come to church' then our mission is simply to invite people to our space and our territory. But we are mistaken if we think that God's mission occurs optimally in the church, on our turf and on our terms.

The mission energy of God the Holy Spirit is more centrifugal than centripetal. Centripetal force attracts into the centre, while centrifugal force sends out from the centre. They are not mutually exclusive concepts but the question here is one of where the emphasis ought to be placed – attracting people in or sending people out.

The reality is that people generally do not want to come and join us. There is no easy way to attract people to Church.

I mentioned in the Introduction that when I was converted, I enthusiastically took Salvation Army literature to public houses on Friday evenings every week – and the challenge of witness there was exciting. Being on their own territory allowed the people I spoke with to set the agenda in surroundings they controlled and were comfortable in. In effect, they made the rules of engagement and I was there as a guest. I needed to be sensitive to that and to spend more time listening than talking.

Most Christians spend a great deal of their time on the ground of the unchurched, but the problem is that they do not necessarily see themselves as disciples or missionaries sent by God. What is important for us to accept is that, when we leave the safe ground of our corps or church, we leave as missionaries – sent by the Father to reveal the Son in the power of the Holy Spirit. That has nothing to do with church-driven programmes – such as visiting the pubs with *The War Cry* – but with an inner conviction, born of the Holy Spirit, that says 'you are sent to share Jesus'. We are the lives in which Jesus is incarnated every day and everywhere we go. We are living letters, a perpetual witness. It seems to me that the most effective evangelism is not what the church organises, but that which happens when Christians engage in witness in their workplaces, colleges and schools, places of leisure and in their neighbourhoods. We know this, of course, but how well equipped are we to share our faith in these settings? How effective are we?

Another important factor to note concerning 'whose turf' is that people are less receptive on church property – if they go into a church at all. US pastor David Womack compared the missionary disciple to a hot-house plant:

> 'The plant must break out of its stained-glass sanctuary and take its life into the open fields. Its seeds must be scattered on the soil of every nation. It must be nurtured, encouraged, turned loose in its wild, uncontrollable state. It must be freed to the force of the wind and the driving rain, for the seed carries in its cells the knowledge of its own destiny. It must take root and bear fruit in every conceivable environment on the face of the planet.'[5]

Perhaps the answer to these questions lies less in mechanics and programmes and more in our own attitudes and reservations. Methods can be taught, attitudes cannot. There is a key distinction between having a missionary attitude and engaging in missionary activity. A corps may engage in missionary activities, such as campaigns or recruiting initiatives, but individuals might be lukewarm and unenthusiastic in their support. The missionary outlook of the believer is the most important factor in the truly missionary corps.

Some corps hold weekly open-air services in busy shopping centres and high streets. They march out of their halls into the streets behind a band and make a Christian witness in their communities. This is undoubtedly a missionary activity, and one which a corps places high value upon. But do the people involved have a missionary attitude? Do they see this as an extension of their personal mission which they have carried into every arena of their lives? Interestingly, relatively few non-playing members of these corps regularly support the activity – it is in the main a function of the band, in spite of sincere efforts to brand it as a 'whole corps' activity. Within the band, again generally speaking, only a few are willing to lay down their instruments and mix with the gathered crowd to share their faith. Of course, many who engage in this activity on a weekly basis do have a sincere missionary attitude, which underpins and complements the activity. However, the danger is that the activity itself can allow people to conceal the fact that their own attitude may be more about keeping a tradition going rather than reaching people with the life-transforming message of Jesus.

If disciples of Jesus were effective, soul-winning witnesses to him in their daily lives we would not be quite so reliant on church-based missionary programmes for growth. Most people become Christians through a relationship with a Christian, not through a church programme.

However excellent they may be, church-based evangelism activities are no substitute for members who are 'on fire' and passionate about sharing their faith in every arena of their lives. Taking a missionary attitude into our Monday-to-Saturday lives is the only means by which church members become missionary in attitude – and as such seek to finish the work Jesus came to earth to do.

Commissioner William Pearson puts his finger on the issue of attitude in his song 'Lord, Give Me More Soul-Saving Love' (*SASB* 609), which is a plea that the Holy Spirit will bring us that quality.

Understanding the mission of God and our privilege in being part of it will lead us to ask ourselves what kind of church and what kind of disciples we need to be in order that his mission is accomplished in and through our lives. We could answer with these words attributed to William Booth:

'While women weep, as they do now, I'll fight; while little children go hungry, as they do now, I'll fight; while men go to prison, in and out, in and out, as they do now, I'll fight; while there is a drunkard left, while there is a poor lost girl upon the streets, while there remains one dark soul without the light of God, I'll fight – I'll fight to the very end!'

CHAPTER FOUR

The Soul-Saving Charism

WE now turn to the dominant Salvation Army charisms, beginning with the charism of soul-saving, which is among the most pressing needs of the Army today. There should be nothing that matters more to Salvationists than to see God's lost children found, reconciled to him and discipled for Christ. We need to be constantly focused on this Kingdom priority. Any progress The Salvation Army makes that does not have soul-saving at the centre of it will not be the kind of progress that ultimately matters – indeed it may not be progress at all. William Booth said he would prefer The Salvation Army to cease to exist if it lost its soul-saving passion. Unless we, as disciples, make disciples, who in turn make disciples, we will not fulfil our divine mandate. Soul-saving is God's priority.

I visited Nigeria in 2007 as a guest lecturer with the International Centre of Learning at Cliff College, the Methodist Bible College. I was asked to give a number of lectures on the subject of evangelism in two Methodist Bible colleges in different parts of that vast country. It was a fascinating experience but what struck me was that the Methodist Church in Nigeria had committed itself to evangelism as its sole priority for the next ten years. The rationale was that if they failed at anything, they surely must not fail in this aspect of their spiritual life and mission.

It is also true to say they were concerned about the declining numbers of Methodists in the country – they were down to around 750,000 in Nigeria at that stage! I met the Bishop whom the Prelate of the Methodist Church had appointed as the Director of Evangelism. He was one of the youngest, brightest and most gifted 'up-and-coming' leaders in that Church. This highly educated, godly man was both articulate and passionate about evangelism. He sat on every board and committee to ensure that evangelism was the lens through which decisions were made and resources allocated and was free to confront any part of the Church that was not placing evangelism at the forefront of its programme.

There was an excitement in the air; a sense that the Church was reconnecting with the mission of God, and that they had a holy expectation that God would bless them. This energy spread itself through the whole organisation throughout the country – laity and clergy alike. The Director of Evangelism adopted the slogan 'Every Methodist An Evangelist', and developed a strategy to train and equip each person, clergy included, to be effective evangelists.

I am not suggesting that we replicate what the Nigerian Methodists were doing, although we could do worse. But it is clear that we need to discover ways in which we can intelligently engage in evangelism in our culture and time, and in so doing align ourselves with God, the Evangelist. I believe that when we do we will see new disciples being made, who in turn will make new disciples and, as a result, we will experience renewal. Once started, the momentum will grow and we will again make a significant impact on our communities – and our nation.

In his discourse with the disciples in John 15, Jesus uses the analogy of the vine bearing much fruit. Some years ago at UK Officers Councils, Commissioner Francy Cachelin conducted a study on this chapter. He talked about the process by which water becomes wine, stating: 'Water becomes wine by going through the vine.' The application was obvious – wine (spiritual fruit) is produced from the water of human life, as a person abides in Christ.

He then talked about what the vine produces and went on to describe how the seed contains the key to reproduction and ongoing life. 'What is the product of the vine?' queried the commissioner. 'Another vine,' was his answer.

This is the natural order of all things that grow and replicate. In the Christian context, disciples should ultimately produce other disciples. Leaders should produce leaders. Corps should produce corps. And so it continues as a reproductive, multiplying cycle of life. Surely, this is what Jesus meant by 'fruit that endures' (v16), that lasts – that we reproduce ourselves or, more accurately, himself.

The Salvation Army must continue to pray even more earnestly that the Holy Spirit will allow us to capture, or recapture, this charism of soul-saving – for we cannot gain it through our own enterprise. The paradox is that a charism is a gift. However, this is one which God wants to renew in us and lavish upon us. After all, this is his mission.

Soul-saving was, and is, foundational to the Army's identity and purpose. This explains both William Booth's own motivation and the unprecedented phenomenal growth of the Movement from its early days. If we were to remove this soul-saving charism from the story, the Army would lose its heartbeat.

The following quote identifies William and Catherine Booth's first love. In a letter to their son Ballington, Catherine, expressing the passion of them both, wrote: 'We want men who are set on soul-saving; who are not ashamed to let everyone know that this is the one aim and object of their life and that they make everything secondary to this.'[1]

The Booths' sole purpose in the early days of their ministry, when William was attached to New Connexion Methodism, was to preach to sinners and see them converted. When he formed The Christian Mission in 1865, William's single focus was that of converting sinners, considering this to be 'the highest service that could be rendered to the poor'[2].

Several other factors from the Army's founding story reinforce our understanding of this charism.

First, the early mottos and slogans reflected this central soul-saving passion. 'Go for souls and go for the worst' outlined the strategy of William Booth's early followers. When the Army expanded into cities, towns and villages, the pioneers would do exactly this and seek out the most depraved persons and often see them converted. If God could change them, God could change anybody, was the philosophy adopted. The testimony of the most notorious rogue or drunkard would be powerful in the community, and the influence of such conversions led to many finding Christ. It was a divinely inspired strategy.

Second, the songs the early Salvationists produced focused on soul-saving. Many of them spoke about the salvation of souls and cast the vision of a world coming to Christ. From an extensive list, here are just a few examples from the songbook: 'Lord, fill my craving heart, with a deep, burning love for souls' (649); 'I want an even, strong desire, I want a calmly fervent zeal, to save poor souls out of the fire' (720); 'All round the world the Army chariot rolls, all round the world the Lord is saving souls' (775).

The vision for 'saving the world' is a recurrent theme in these early songs. This is quite remarkable when we consider that most of those early Salvationists would have never, in the whole of their lives, travelled beyond a few miles from their home and work environments. Also, newspapers and media communication, which we take for granted, were nothing like they are today. Nevertheless, an immense vision of 'the world for God' dominated the collective thinking of these early Salvationists.

Third, the very name William Booth gave to the Movement, The Salvation Army, clearly announces the emphasis on the saving mission. We recall the account of the discussion between the early founders about how The Christian Mission could be described. The phrase 'volunteer Army' was first suggested, but it was overruled and changed to 'Salvation Army', which in their view was a clearer expression of the purpose and goal of the Movement.

Finally, the incredible number of souls saved or the number of people who were converted through the ministry of The Salvation Army bears witness to its primary objective. General John Larsson documents the early success of The Salvation Army: 'The Salvation Army did not begin with a big bang. By early 1878, after 13 years of plodding growth as The Christian Mission, it had only 30 stations and 36 evangelists to show for its labours.'

He then goes on to speak of the dramatic change when The Salvation Army was founded in 1878:

> 'The results were spectacular by any standard. By the end of the year the number of stations had doubled and the number of evangelists trebled. By 1886, eight years later, there were 1,006 corps in Britain and 2,260 officers – a growth rate of 3,300 per cent and 6,200 per cent respectively.'[3]

This evidence (and there is much more) supports the claim that soul-saving was a charism of The Salvation Army's founders. The question for us now is: How do we claim this in a 21st-century context?

Retrieving the soul-saving charism

Before going any further, we must define what we actually mean by 'soul-saving'. Although it is a rather old-fashioned term, I have chosen it for two reasons. First, it resonates with our Salvation Army heritage. Second, as we have seen, the current UK Territory Mission Statement declares boldly that, as disciples of Jesus Christ, The Salvation Army exists to 'save souls'.

For the sake of clarity, let me state unequivocally that soul-saving is not just about making converts, although obviously that is involved. We are talking about everything that goes into making devoted disciples of Jesus Christ. Soul-saving should be understood as making disciples, and not merely making converts. The difference is vital.

In the early 1990s, Martin Robinson, Principal of Springdale College, Birmingham, told a group of Salvation Army officers that it takes at least two years to make a disciple. However, on further investigation into Church history, it seems that even two years is quite short when compared to the disciple-making process in the very early Church, where it often took a great deal longer for a convert to be accepted in the Christian community as a disciple of Jesus. The process was known as catechesis. This thorough instruction took converts from the very early stage of enquiry right through to fully developed, mature discipleship. Converts would be taught all the spiritual disciplines of praying, studying the Bible, worshipping, fasting, giving, witnessing, repentance and growth into holiness, that is, Christlikeness. It was at the end of a long process, when the individual had satisfactorily demonstrated to the church leaders their obedience to and faith in Christ, that they took their place in the body of believers and were able to call themselves fully-fledged Christians.

The relevance of all of this is that we, too, need to give careful thought as to how we make disciples in the 21st-century Salvation Army. More important than how many disciples we are making are the questions: 'What kind of disciples are we making? ' and 'How well-resourced are they for soul-saving?'

Consumer disciples

One important factor that significantly impacts soul-saving is whether our own proclivity towards Christian faith, lifestyle and witness is as consumers or as missionaries. Is our disposition one that takes or gives? Disciples are disposed to the latter. According to Jesus, discipleship is about losing one's life in order to gain life (Mark 8:35). As disciples, we are called to live out the principle of laying down our lives daily, so that others can pick up theirs.

Why is it, then, that we have developed a Church culture in which it seems that 20% of our congregations engage in the ministry, while 80% are spectators who are passive in their discipleship and never participate? They watch others from the safe distance of non-involvement, justifying their position by either claiming to have nothing to offer, or of having never been asked. They do not seem to be aware that God asks his followers, as he asked Isaiah: 'Whom shall I send? Who will be our messenger?' (Isaiah 6:8). Isaiah's response was: 'I will go! Send me!'

One possible reason for this passivity is that the 80% are in consumer mode; they are non-participating spectators. They want worship that entertains, preaching that is over quickly and that contains little or no personal challenge to change – but neither must it be boring nor fail to deliver a 'buzz' to the listener. Consumers want financial giving that is kept at a token level, rather than one that involves tithe and sacrifice. They accept involvement and participation as long as it does not disturb their weekly schedule or lifestyle, and claim the right to select from religion what suits their lives and is convenient to them. In his book *The Forgotten Ways*, missiologist Alan Hirsch hits the nail on the head when he says: 'I have come to the dreaded conclusion that we simply cannot consume our way into discipleship.'[4]

The idol of consumerism in our culture claims that we can choose and have whatever we want. We fall for the hollow but persuasive myth that we can spend our way to pleasure and happiness and find fulfilment and joy. The life of the disciple is not shaped by these values. Consumerism has no place in radical discipleship. Disciples of Jesus demonstrate the capacity to live in a way that defies the prevailing culture and points people towards the richness of a Christ-centred life, in which we have everything we need.

Thus, the first challenge, in terms of retrieving the charism of soul-saving in the 21st century, is to reflect on our own attitude to the prevailing culture in which we live. Is it squeezing us into its mould, or are we living as counter-cultural, radical disciples of Jesus? In this consumer-driven age, we as disciples willingly give up our right to make our own choices, surrendering to a higher choice which is God's will for us. Our 'whole of life' choice is that Jesus is Lord. He calls us to take him into every corner of our world. Therefore, the stark and most challenging question in the business of soul-saving may not be 'How do I do it?', but 'Do I really want to?'

Resourcing disciples

The Army that I read about in Richard Collier's book *The General Next to God* was the Army whose missionary philosophy was 'if they won't come in and join us, we'll go out to them'. We need to find new ways to do that and to infiltrate our communities with Christlike, holy saints. This was the early Army way.

We have always been a 'sent' Army. William Booth's masterpiece of a book *In Darkest England and the Way Out* is essentially about Christians getting out and engaging with a fallen world. It is about disciples of Jesus venturing out into the dangerous darkness, as vulnerable witnesses, going into slums, prisons, beer halls, ghettos, street corners and boldly taking Christ's gospel with them. Booth created a powerful image of Christians risking their own safety by reaching down from the security of the rock in order to grab the lost from the sea of hell. This does not correlate with an 'attractional' model of evangelism which is inevitably done from the safe haven of the Church. The Salvation Army is a church willing to take the risk and go to where the people are.

We will be no use if we simply live together with fellow believers in holy isolation. People will not catch the Christian 'bug' unless they are exposed to it. The fact that relatively few people do come and join us, or catch the bug, does not seem to add any urgency to the requirement to do what we should be doing – getting out there making ourselves wildly infectious – or contagious. We should 'sneeze' the bug, suggests Hirsch, over the entire population. Bill Hybels, founder of Willow Creek Community Church, also develops this theme with his excellent training resource *Becoming a Contagious Christian*.

We need to find new ways to 'go'. I dream of leading a congregation where every worshipper leaves the sanctuary as a missionary, a sent evangelist. Thus we penetrate every corner of our community with sent missionary disciples who use all their time, at work, in leisure activity, in every contact with people, to make Jesus real and live for the purpose of getting others to know him.

I once watched a DVD about a teacher whose church had decided to make her the Sunday school leader – her teaching and relational skills with children seemingly made her an obvious choice for this role. The church invited her to the front for prayer and for the ceremony of making her the leader in front of the congregation. She was not terribly impressed. Here is the gist of what she said:

> 'Why has the church never invited me to the front for prayer before? I have been teaching in front of classes of 30-40 kids for over 15 years. These are not Sunday school or kids with supportive Christian families, and yet the church never once thought to pray for my teaching them. Now they want me to teach 15 church kids for 40 minutes once a week and I'm the prayer focus! What's more important – our kids in church or those kids I meet in school every day where I go to live out my faith in non-church environment?'[5]

She had a point. What do our churches do to resource people who are sent out to the world every week into many places where they are witnesses? Surely this is what it means to be a missionary church engaged in the mission of God – resourcing, equipping and praying for our people as they take their part in his mission in the world.

The effective part of any corps 'soul-saving programme' is unwritten and not timetabled. It is dominated by faith-sharing interactions as the congregation disperses and penetrates the community. These interactions happen in informal meetings in people's homes and between neighbours, in shops, restaurants, leisure centres and just about anywhere else where you can get someone to stand still long enough to listen to the story of Jesus. I know one person who looks for opportunities to share his faith in Jesus with those who deliver services to his house. I remember thinking that the poor post delivery person doesn't stand a chance! The gospel gets incarnated all over the neighbourhood.

Incarnational evangelism

We looked at the concept of 'being sent' when we considered the mission of God (Chapter 3) and we now look at it in the context of incarnational evangelism. Incarnation, as defined in the prologue of John's Gospel, is about God moving 'into the neighbourhood' (see John 1:14 *The Message*). The mystery of the Word becoming flesh, Jesus coming to earth and living among us, is mind-blowing.

To commence his book John selects the words 'In the beginning', and in doing so reminds us that the story of Jesus is the Genesis story and the creation of time and the cosmos. In Jesus, says John, we discover that the origins and goals of God's purposes in the universe find their existence and fulfilment. John presents Jesus as the 'sent' Word – sent into our neighbourhood to be with us, and to be one of us. In his incarnation, Jesus genuinely identifies with us by taking on our humanity, and we witness that God is revealed in his life. We recognise grace, truth and glory. We see and understand a God who is one of us, who knows and loves us and shows us the way.

Leonard Sweet cleverly boils the Prologue (John 1:1-14) down to two words: 'Be there.' 'Be' refers to the identity, the mystery of Christ, the Word, while 'there' refers to the locality, the neighbourhood the Word moved into.

Here's the challenge to the church that wants to recapture the soul-saving charism: move into the neighbourhood while retaining your identity. Don't be there and become like them, advises Sweet. Be there and be like Jesus, which is the missional challenge of holy living. As we accept the challenge, the 'revelation' impact of incarnational evangelism will happen. People will see Christ – in us. This is the highest ambition for the soul winner.

Alan Hirsch suggests four dimensions that constitute incarnational evangelism – presence, proximity, powerlessness and proclamation[6]. We can explore each of these in a Salvation Army context.

Presence

A great deal of The Salvation Army's mission relies on our 'being there' – or presence evangelism – often at the sharp end of human need and suffering, disasters and emergencies. The old slogan 'Where there's a need, there's The Salvation Army' reinforces the denominational commitment to being there.

What is noteworthy from Jesus' time on earth is that, for the first 30 years, no one noticed his presence. After his baptism by John, his mission was more public and aggressive. But for the early years he lived in relative anonymity. This reminds us that incarnational evangelism can often be unremarkable as we simply 'be there' and let our presence be the influence over the long haul.

Jesus was quite comfortable with people and he loved to be in the company of those from different backgrounds. People got the impression from their encounters with Jesus that he actually liked them and could not spend enough time with them. How would we fare? Do we enjoy being with the people we are sent to reach, listening to them, learning about them and from them?

I am reminded again of Bill Hybels who is so serious about reaching people in the community that he has studied them intensively. His church used Lee Strobel's book *Unchurched Harry and Mary*, about two fictitious people, to devise a seven-step strategy on how to get 'Harry' and 'Mary' to meet Christ, become disciples and then mature in their new life in Christ. The first step of the strategy was that someone from the church needed to go, build a relationship with Harry and Mary and get to know and love them.

Our challenge is to find ways of being there – of penetrating our communities in every way possible. If it means holding some worship meetings and activities in schools or community centres, getting involved in local politics or school governing bodies, joining sports and leisure clubs or interest groups, organising social events that attract neighbours and friends, or taking part in neighbourhood/ residents groups – we should be there.

Proximity

Jesus identified with the poor, the excluded and the suffering. It is also true that he met with the rich, the religious and the successful. He managed to connect with people and give them a sense that they were valued. However, this is particularly true of the broken and the lost whom the religious establishment had contrived to exclude. I am reminded here of the work of William Booth and the early Salvation Army. I recall the story of Bramwell Booth and W. T. Stead who, when dealing with the issue of prostitution among the very young, challenged the law over the age of consent in Britain – and found themselves arrested for their efforts.

William Booth's proximity to and identification with the poor resulted in innovative projects that brought glory to God and gave him a credible platform from which to witness to Christ, who could ultimately transform those situations. His pragmatism in providing shelter when he encountered people who had no food or place to stay, writing *In Darkest England and the Way Out* and formulating the Cab Horse Charter (see Chapter 6) were all conceived from his proximity to, and love for, the poor and his determination to fight against the conditions that paralyse people through injustice and oppression.

Powerlessness

The powerlessness that incarnational living brings takes the patronage out of evangelism. It dismisses the arrogance of 'we're better than you'; or, even worse, the implicit message that 'we're saved and you're not'. Incarnational evangelism is birthed in a stable away from the spotlight or limelight. It is a light that gently and quietly shines.

Incarnational evangelism listens more than it speaks. It learns more than it teaches. It serves more than it demands. It is marked more by humility and grace than by attainment and accomplishment.

It is always a sad thing to see evangelism executed from a dominating and condescending stance. Could it be that such a stance has prevented us from reaching out to different ethnicities and races? Cross-cultural evangelism is partly about bridge-building – that is, two-way bridges, built to be crossed by both groups so they connect. How can we both build and cross bridges into other communities and offer Christ to them? This is a challenge we will increasingly need to embrace in our multicultural society. What does it mean to be a light to the nations when the nations live next door to us?

Proclamation

Presence evangelism needs to be followed up with proclamation. This means that the gospel story must be communicated. Andrew Walker, Senior Lecturer in Theology at King's College, London, points out in his book *Telling the Story* that Britons live in a society where the story of Jesus is simply not known to an increasing number of people. If it is known, it is one among many. He argues that the Church needs to find new ways of sharing the story of Jesus so that it can once again become hope for the world.

When we tell the gospel story, do we take time to listen to and value people's personal beliefs and world view? In his book *The Faith of the Unbeliever*, British writer Martin Robinson states: 'Unbelief in any kind of God is very much a minority position across all the groups.'[7]

As the title of Robinson's book suggests, people do have beliefs and, before they listen to anything we have to say, they will need to feel that they have been understood. This is about respect, where our need to be heard is secondary to their need to be understood. When people feel they have been listened to they may be disposed to hear the story we have to share.

Not everyone will accept the story, but that ought not to prevent us from telling it and celebrating it every time we possibly can.

In conclusion, an incarnational approach to soul-saving will require us to be authentic in our living. Martyn Atkins, General Secretary of the Methodist Church, puts together some helpful phrases in his book *Resourcing Renewal*:

- Being comes before doing (but 'doing' is not optional).

- Lives and lips are in agreement (living it and telling it are indissoluble).

- Being vulnerable is as important as being strong.

- Being real is better than always being right.

- Being close is better than being distant.

- Travelling together on the journey is as important as arriving together.

- Inviting people to believe is inviting people to belong (and vice versa).[8]

The question is: to what extent are we prepared to identify ourselves with, and become an intrinsic part of, our own community as Christ's living witnesses?

There is, quite rightly, a great deal of emphasis placed on incarnational evangelism these days. It depends on the building of genuine relationships where the value and outcomes of these relationships, in an evangelistic sense, cannot be measured merely by addition. Numerical growth cannot be the only, or main, measure for 'success' in evangelism. The church growth models that measure effectiveness in this way are flawed because relationship evangelism is much more open-ended and unpredictable and, therefore, difficult to quantify.

When we start counting numbers, we miss the point. There was no guarantee that the vast swathes of people whom Jesus encountered in his ministry would join in his mission – indeed one could argue that the relatively small number of disciples (12) and followers (up to 120) constitute failure in numerical measuring terms. For Jesus, 'being there' was enough. It was through incarnation that God was able to accomplish his redemptive purposes in the world and, since Christ came to earth, millions in every age have found salvation through Jesus. At our best, we, his disciples, will follow his lead as we seek to live out the soul-saving charism.

CHAPTER FIVE

The Holiness Charism

HOLINESS is a crucial, continuous acquisition of grace for the disciple of Jesus, according to William Booth. Booth's official biographer Harold Begbie writes:

> 'His emphasis was on conversion, the conversion of the adult and intelligent individual, and this was the first and greatest of his preachings. But beyond the arrest of the sinner, and the awakening of the soul to the living fact of a living God, lay the path of holiness, and here William Booth could not stop and leave conversion to follow its own evolution.'[1]

We have looked at the soul-saving charism and now, following the order laid out in General John Gowans's mission statement, we come to growing saints – the holiness charism.

In the book *Salvation Soldiery*, a compilation of his sermons, Booth writes with his usual passion about the subject and articulates his earnest desire that every Christian should know and experience holiness in his or her own life, saying: 'Holiness to the Lord is to us a fundamental truth; it stands in the front rank of our doctrines.'[2]

In this sermon he outlines how a person should understand holiness and then receive holiness. He views it as an imperative for

Salvationists and crucial to their effectiveness in the salvation war: 'Holiness is indispensable to your completest usefulness.'[3]

Although Booth believed that soul-saving and conversion were of eternal importance, he taught that conversion alone falls short of everything God wants to accomplish in human life. He emphasised in his proclamation of the gospel that the path of holiness was a crucial characteristic in the life of all new disciples. So much so that the dual message of the gospel, salvation and holiness, became the watchword and motto, 'Blood And Fire', for The Salvation Army. 'Blood' symbolises the redeeming sacrifice of Christ. 'Fire' represents the sanctifying power of the Holy Spirit.

Begbie recognised the charism in William Booth's ministry that called people to complete commitment to holiness of life:

'Although William Booth had decided that the Christian Mission should set before itself the task of arousing the indifference of the apathetic, and of converting the sunken and depraved sinner, he was still immensely conscious of the need for spiritual growth in holiness. His one tendency towards mysticism lay in this direction, and unless we perfectly acquaint ourselves with the character of this tendency we shall miss the secret of his inner life.'[4]

This 'tendency towards mysticism' both balanced and brought a sense of completion to William Booth's soul-saving, revivalist charism. For Booth, the messages of soul-saving and holiness of life were foundational to the mission of The Salvation Army.

Through the charism of holiness, Booth and the founding members were bound together with an incredible unity and focus of purpose. They were collectively energised to execute God's 'Blood And Fire' mission. As new converts claimed holiness of life, this somehow continuously fuelled the ongoing soul-saving mission with more and more converts being won and discipled for Christ. The mystery of how this charism galvanised the early Army community, and not just William Booth as an individual, is difficult to describe. However, in reality it did just that and is further evidence of the creative and providential workings of the Holy Spirit during that time of formation.

If a movement receives a charism, then the whole movement affirms it in its corporate acceptance of and witness to it. This is the natural consequence of the founder's and the founding leadership's embracement of it. This adds force to the evidence that holiness is a charism bestowed upon The Salvation Army, precisely because it is reflected and promoted in the lives of those who became part of the early community of Salvationists.

It is interesting to note that, in early Salvation Army hierarchy, the holiness charism was eagerly championed, not only by William Booth, but also by other pioneer leaders. For example, Commissioner Samuel Logan Brengle became the best known of the Army's holiness teachers. Brengle was passionate about holiness and wrote a number of books which are still used both inside and outside the Army. His holiness volumes are generally considered to be classics.

We can confidently state that William Booth's passion for holiness resonated with his followers. It was not only a personal experience for him, but one which consecrated the early Salvation Army community.

We also know that in receiving a charism a prophetic figure speaks to his or her present age with foresight and the wisdom of God. To some extent the effectiveness of this can only be fully assessed with the benefit of hindsight. However, one would expect future generations to affirm and confirm that the messenger and message were authentic and Holy Spirit-initiated.

There is plenty of supporting evidence that subsequent generations of Salvationists prioritised the holiness charism. One is the numerous books that have since been written on the subject, and indeed are still being written. The writings of various Generals have sharpened the focus on holiness teaching. Frederick Coutts wrote two excellent books on the subject called *The Doctrine of Holiness* and *The Call to Holiness* while John Larsson gives fresh emphasis in his book *The Man Perfectly Filled with the Spirit*. Shaw Clifton has written widely on the subject; his book *New Love: Thinking about Practical Holiness* is a collection of essays by Salvationist writers who set out to reaffirm the practical, day-by-day relevance of the Army's holiness teaching.

All these writers evidence the passion that William Booth and the early Salvationists had for holiness. This yearning has been a reality for Salvationists in every generation. As General Larsson's introduction states:

> 'This is a book for those who yearn to be more like their Lord and Master Jesus Christ. It is for those dissatisfied with themselves as they are and who want to know how their lives might reflect more of the radiant nature and spiritual effectiveness of the Man from Nazareth.'[5]

Other Salvationist writers have also made their contribution. Chick Yuill's *We Need Saints* is an exposition of holiness, in which he writes of the charism being renewed in each generation. He hits the nail on the head when he says: 'Each new generation of Christians, while owing much to those who have gone before, must face the task of reinterpreting vital Christian truth for its own age.'[6]

There are three further areas which confirm that the holiness charism has indeed travelled down the path of succeeding Salvation Army generations and adapted itself within every era.

First, Brengle Institutes have been established in nearly every part of the world. These institutes are a form of spiritual retreat for those who wish to explore the Bible's teaching on holiness and thus personally renew their understanding and experience of holiness at a deeper level.

Second, the holiness meeting has been an enduring focus in corps around the world. This early-day institution encourages biblical teaching on holiness of life as a central tenet of Salvationism.

Third, this charism is present in our tenth Salvation Army doctrine and thus provides further strong evidence of the ownership of the charism within the Salvation Army community: 'We believe that it is the privilege of all believers to be wholly sanctified, and that their whole spirit, soul and body may be preserved blameless unto the coming of our Lord Jesus Christ.'

There is no doubt that this emphasis on the appropriation of holiness gave the early Salvationists a credible platform on which to preach Christ and thus qualify them to serve suffering humanity. The identification of holiness as a charism for the Army seems to pass every test. It is a work of the Holy Spirit in the life of the Founder which found a resonance with the early members of the Movement. It fulfils aspects of Christ's purpose in the world in terms of identity and mission and it is a unique gift 'for the common good' as it affects how Christians live in relation to others.

Holiness is essential to the mission of God. The Bible is a story of a missionary God. He is the God who created the cosmos, the earth and its people. Things went wrong and have been put right by means of his redemptive plan, carried out in his Son, Jesus Christ. The Church of God is created for the mission of God. God's mission calls for, and seeks, a human response. That response is holiness.

The 21st-century context

Where does God get his credibility? How does he get a hearing? God's reputation in the world depends on us living holy lives. Therefore, the charism of holiness requires constant renewal in our lives. This will keep the focus where it rightly belongs. The primary purpose of holiness is not personal piety but that our lives demonstrate to others what God is like – that we become different and distinct in a way that reflects who God is. They will then want to know and experience his love for themselves. 'You shall be holy and belong only to me, because I am the Lord and I am holy' (Leviticus 20:26).

In *The Mission of God* Langham Partnership's Christopher Wright reminds us that holiness is both indicative and imperative[7]. That is to say, it is indicative in that holiness is God-given and God-initiated. It was God who set Israel apart and made the nation holy (Leviticus 22:32). God sanctifies – that is he makes us holy – by conferring his holiness on us.

Having accepted holiness as a gift from God, the imperative is that we are then challenged to live it out in the world. It is as if God says: 'I have made you holy, now go and be who you are and live with personal integrity and compassion towards the poor and suffering and strive for justice.'

Having understood the missionary context of holiness, we now need to reflect on how it fits into the context of modern living. Were we to read Brengle's timeless volumes we would find the material remains relevant and of value in every generation. Nevertheless, we can add further value by speaking into our own context and try better to envision what holiness, Christlikeness, will look like in our multifaceted 21st-century lives.

We can do this through the lens of 'relationship', which we have already seen is vital for incarnational mission. Here we will explore four facets – the relationships we have with God, with our inner self, with others and with our environment.

Relationship with God
Because of what Jesus did for us in terms of restoring our relationship with a loving heavenly Father, we are able to have a personal relationship of deep intimacy with God. We can deepen that relationship through prayer. Jesus talked about the place of prayer (Matthew 6:6) where we meet and interact with God in secret, as opposed to the public arena. It has been said: 'The secret of praying, is praying in secret.' People who live their lives solely in the public domain rob themselves of authenticity and of the blessing of being in the presence of God in private.

The relationship between private and public religion attracted a good deal of comment from Jesus in the Gospels. He pointed out that gaps between these domains represented the beginning of hypocrisy – as in the case of the Pharisees, who loved to make a public show of their religion (see Matthew 23:5-7). If we are committed to serving God in our corps, in whatever capacity, and do not engage in regular, private communion with our Father, we are in danger of becoming hypocrites. We cannot be in public what we are not in private. Years ago, George Campbell Morgan, pastor of Westminster Chapel, London, explained this using the concept of a circle, saying it has a centre and a circumference and that no one can draw a perfect circumference without being anchored at the centre – by using a compass. Morgan went on to say that we cannot draw the circumference of our lives (the public arena) without first nailing the centre. This can only be done in a secret space where we meet with God. Holiness is about living a centred life: Christ-centred.

It remains challenging for many of us to find the time and space where we can commune intimately with God on a regular basis. Yet we must persist if we are to be authentic and effective as disciples.

Relationship with our inner world
In this day and age, there are myriad devious, subtle challenges to our inner world. Temptations come to us in forms unknown to our parents and grandparents, particularly through the internet and other media. There are temptations seldom spoken about that hold powerful potential for the destruction of the inner self. Some can even become addictions that enslave and trap individuals in a lonely torment. The call to holiness is a call to purity whereby we overcome these enticements and maintain the integrity of the inner self.

The first area of our inner life worthy of consideration here concerns our own self-worth. Jesus told us that we must lose our life if we are to find it (Matthew 10:39). Paul speaks of dying to self: 'I have died, but Christ lives in me. And I now live by faith in the Son of God, who loved me and gave his life for me' (Galatians 2:20 *CEV*).

55

While extolling the benefits of the Christian faith, for example, we must not lose sight of the crucial importance of losing ourselves – even dying to ourselves. Popular psychology tells us to become our own gods. As Christians, we find ourselves by losing ourselves in the Lordship of Jesus Christ. It is as we allow him to live his life in us that we live and discover a self that is found by no other means than self-surrender. Alison Elliot, former Moderator of the Church of Scotland's General Assembly, says:

> 'Most of us want success and so achieve nothing. Jesus made himself nothing and so achieved abiding success. Most of us suppress our past and so pretend a future. Jesus was prepared to sacrifice his future to give us hope for our past. Most of us are tempted to use people and lose all respect. Jesus won respect by being willing to let others make use of him.'

To make Jesus 'Lord of me', by crucifying self, takes us along a path where we discover a brand new inner life in Christ. It is in Christ that we find our true selves.

The second area for reflection is that of personal wealth. In a consumer-driven society it is important for us to model detachment from that culture and demonstrate generosity in the use of our wealth – whether we have little or much. What, if anything, prevents us from at least tithing as an indication that Jesus is Lord of our finances? As we release our money we release more and more of that egocentric self and its potential for greed. We let go of our reliance on false security that wealth promises. In a spirit of thanksgiving we as disciples hold our money lightly. When we receive we do not grab, and when we let go, we do so freely. After all, we are not the owners of what we give.

Then we must reflect on the issue of the internet and the potential it has to enslave individuals in destructive behaviours. For example, there is an addictive power to internet pornography. A recent TV documentary highlighted and exposed this in the lives of people as young as 13-14 years of age. I suspect that more people than we imagine are struggling with this relentless temptation, making their inner lives miserable. This is not just a problem in the inner life of an individual, of course. Such behaviour, however secret, pervades the whole of life. It negatively impacts marriages and attitudes to sex; it reinforces the sex industry and traps the vulnerable in it. It objectifies women and children, degrading them as God's created and loved people.[8]

Holiness involves our thinking. Paul in his writings encourages us to '... take every thought captive and make it obey Christ' (2 Corinthians 10:5).

Purity of heart is the beginning of the journey towards holiness. The pure in heart get to see God, and they are blessed (see Matthew 5:8).

Relationship with others

The supreme commandment given by Jesus that governs our relationships is 'Love one another'. Indeed Jesus summed up all the commandments in answer to a question from a Pharisee:

> '"Teacher, what is the most important commandment in the Law?" Jesus answered: Love the Lord your God with all your heart, soul, and mind. This is the first and most important commandment. The second most important commandment is like this one. And it is, "Love others as much as you love yourself"' (Matthew 22:36-39 CEV).

How sad it is when we encounter fellowships where this has been forgotten and relationships are anything but loving! Instead, suspicion, bitterness, gossip and envy characterise the culture. This elementary aspect of our corporate life is severely undertaught and under-practised. Our activity-based, task-orientated fellowships deprive us of space and time to 'be' with one another.

We could do with developing a more robust theology of what loving one another means and creating new models of what a 'love-one-another' fellowship really looks like. There is something very powerful about a community of God's people who live this out, work it out and demonstrate it together.

However, this is extremely difficult. It involves humility, forgiveness, accountability, patience and the willingness to be vulnerable, open and honest – and it is going to be just as tough in the Church as anywhere else. We don't always find it easy to forgive those who hurt us, especially if they show no remorse. If we are going to do relationships in the 'I love you' way we need to 'unlearn' things that may be spoiling our church culture and learn to be different.

Here are a few pointers to consider.

First, let's not speak negatively about others in their absence. If we enjoy fellowship with others at church, we want to know that they will have a sense of loyalty to us when we are absent – and vice versa. This is the basis of trust. In some circumstances we may need to discuss other people, for example, whether they are suitable for leadership. In those conversations, what we share should be motivated by concern for that person's highest good and not by any negative reasons.

Second, let's learn what forgiveness really means. One of the best books I can recommend on this subject is *Total Forgiveness* by R. T. Kendall, former pastor of Westminster Chapel in London. Totally forgiving is not totally forgetting, he writes. It is remembering without bitterness. When we truly forgive we wipe clean the bitterness that can destroy us. It means letting go and understanding what it means to be truly vulnerable. This is the road to healing. Easy? No. Possible? Gloriously, through God's grace.

Third, let's focus church life on relationships rather than tasks. Is it possible to properly be 'church' without small groups in which relationships flourish? I don't believe it is. We need to intentionally

58

create arenas for *koinonia* – what the New Testament describes as fellowship.

Relationship with the environment

There is a growing response among the churches in Britain to the challenge of our relationship with the environment. The Methodist, Baptist and United Reformed Church joint working group has produced a report called *Hope in God's Future: Christian Discipleship in the Context of Climate Change*. The focus is on the impact that climate change is having on the world's poorest people.

Interestingly, the Army's 2010 Helping-Hand Project featured climate change under the title Earth: Love People. Love The Earth, raising awareness of this issue in corps along with a significant sum of money. Commissioner Robin Dunster, then Chief of the Staff, declared in an issue of *Salvationist*: 'Of all people, we who are Christians have a mandate, an obligation, to demonstrate our concern in intentional action.'[9]

There are a number of ways to act on environmental issues, both individually and corporately. In our homes we can be aware of the need for recycling and support local government. We can also encourage those in our fellowships to be active within their own communities. Most local councils are producing information on recycling and how residents can access local amenities.

Then there are questions to be asked about Salvation Army property – headquarters buildings, houses, halls and centres. Should any strategy for new buildings be more environmentally inclined? Obviously cost becomes an issue when we start to talk about renewable sources of heating, emissions, carbon footprints and so on. However, this a price that needs to be considered if we are to give more than lip service to this increasingly vital issue.

We can encourage the use of low-energy light bulbs, and recycle more of our communal waste. We can adopt a fair-trade policy in our coffee shops and use environmentally friendly equipment in our offices and kitchens. We can stop printing so many weekly news-sheets when technology allows us to project information onto screens and send them by email.

To sum up, our relationships determine who and what we are. Holiness is as much about 'we' as it is about 'me', but most of all it is about 'he'. We cannot truly and properly be ourselves until he is Lord – and we are one with him (and with each other).

Christopher Wright lists for us the down-to-earth issues that reflect God's holiness from Leviticus Chapter 19:

- respect within the family and community (vv3,32)

- exclusive loyalty to Yahweh as God; proper treatment of sacrifices (vv4,5-8)

- economic generosity in agriculture (vv9-10)

- observing the commandments regarding social relation-ships (vv11-12)

- economic justice in employment rights (v13)

- social compassion to the disabled (v14)

- judicial integrity in the legal system (vv12,15)

- neighbourly attitudes and behaviour; loving one's neighbour as oneself (vv16-18)

- preserving the symbolic tokens of religious distinctiveness (v19)

- sexual integrity (vv20-22,29)

- rejection of practices connected with idolatrous or occult religion (vv26-31)

- no ill-treatment of ethnic minorities, but rather racial equality before the law and practical love for the alien as for oneself (vv33-34)

- commercial honesty in all trading transactions (vv35-36)[10]

This pragmatic and down-to-earth approach to 'whole of life holiness' is completely compatible with a sleeves-rolled-up Salvation Army.

Viewing holiness through the lens of our relationship with God, with our inner self, with others and with our environment helps us understand who God is and that he created us to be like him. We are reminded that the concept of the charism of holiness reflects our concept of God – and that it is intensely practical.

CHAPTER SIX

The Serve Suffering Humanity Charism

THE Salvation Army is arguably best known in the public domain for its commitment to social justice and programmes of social action. Around the world, respect and admiration for the Movement's 'sleeves rolled up' pragmatic expression of Christianity gives it its place as a trusted organisation.

The Army's call to 'serve suffering humanity' is a fundamental aspect of its response to the mission of God. In this chapter I will refer to this aspect as one part of the 'dual mission' of evangelism and social action. This duality does not imply two separate missions; rather they are two sides of the single coin that is the 'mission of God'.

A glimpse into history

William Booth knew about 'suffering humanity' from personal experience. His father lost everything when William was a teenager and he was brought up in abject poverty. 'There is no indication from any of the biographers of Booth that this period of his life was marked by anything other than poverty, and the nineteenth year of his life was the lowest point of this time,' writes Professor Roger Green, a Salvationist.[1]

We have already noted that William Booth was a revivalist preacher with a passion for soul-winning. However, as The

Salvation Army developed from its beginnings in London's East End he was challenged to think deeply about his single emphasis on salvation preaching, when many of his converts were suffering from social injustices as a result of poverty. These new converts had no advocate or means of escape from their dire social and economic conditions. Booth realised that the message of salvation should lead to transformation in the whole of life. His theology underwent a profound challenge and significant change, says Green:

> 'The critical change in the theology of William Booth came when his doctrine of salvation took on social dimensions. In his later theology of redemption, salvation was not only individual, personal and spiritual. Salvation was also social and physical.'[2]

William Booth's response to these social and physical aspects of an individual's salvation led to the early Army's involvement in a phenomenal programme of social action. This occurred alongside his continued evangelistic emphasis, which never diminished.

The evidence that Booth's passion for the poor can be identified as a charism and not merely a 'humanitarian' reaction can be demonstrated in three ways.

First, William Booth was distinctly called by God to his destiny as the Founder of The Salvation Army and God worked in him and through him to develop the Army's mission to reach others with the gospel. Booth's relationship with God informed his relationship with others.

The salvation message in the Bible states that in Christ the whole of creation would be redeemed and healed (see Romans 8:16ff). William Booth came to realise that salvation had social dimensions as well. He found he was unable to ignore the injustice and suffering of the masses of people around him, many of whom were responding to the gospel he was preaching.

Second, charisms are not only recognised and affirmed as private gifts in an individual, they are also given for the good of the whole community. In order for these gifts to be described as charisms we must be able to measure their positive outcomes in the world. *In Darkest England and the Way Out* lays out not just the theological foundation for Booth's social work, but a practical plan as to how the poor could be helped out of their poverty and squalor. His Cab Horse Charter was a clever and insightful piece of social work. The rationale was based on the fact that if every cab horse in London had three basic necessities guaranteed – shelter for the night, food for its stomach and work allotted to it by which it could earn its corn – then how much more should human beings have their basic needs met. Booth's aim was to elevate the conditions of the 'submerged tenth' of the population that was worse off than the cab horses.

Third, do we find reflections of the life of Jesus and his disciples? The Methodist Church's Martyn Atkins once conducted an experiment with a group of around one hundred Salvation Army officers. He asked them to find in the Gospels a text that identifies The Salvation Army and distinguishes its unique mission. After some considerable discussion and debate, the officers agreed on Luke 4:18-19, where Jesus quotes Isaiah:

> 'The Spirit of the Lord is upon me, because he has chosen me to bring good news to the poor. He has sent me to proclaim liberty to the captives and recovery of sight to the blind, to set free the oppressed and announce that the time has come when the Lord will save his people.'

The strong social justice element in the announcement of Jesus as to his mission clearly resonates with Salvationists in the 21st century. This corporate passion has a strong scriptural foundation. The Bible makes it clear that it is the love and justice of God that causes him to be concerned for the poor. The injustices that lead to poverty, oppression, suffering and exclusion disadvantage them. Their pain and suffering is manifested physically, spiritually, sociologically and psychologically and, as a result, God lovingly responds to them.

Who are the poor to whom Jesus refers in the Gospels? Robin Gamble, author of *The Irrelevant Church*, writes:

> 'The collective term "the poor" covers the hungry, the unemployed, the sick, the discouraged, the sad and suffering. The poor are the subjected, oppressed and humiliated people (*ochlos*). The poor are sick, crippled, homeless (Luke 14:21-23). They are the beggars in the streets and on the country roads (Matthew 11:2-5). They are the sad (Luke 6:21).'[3]

Jesus' life and teaching

One of the most striking aspects of Jesus' ministry is his identification with the poor. That is to say, he did not simply act as an agent *for* them, he was one *of* them. We see Jesus coming into the world as a baby, in humility and poverty, not to mention the stench and filth of a stable. Later, because of the hatred of King Herod, the family fled and became refugees in Egypt. We know his parents were poor; in his adulthood, Jesus lived without wealth and had few possessions, apart from his seamless robe. He had no permanent home or land.

His teaching about possessions, treasure and materialism made it clear that he understood the potentially idolatrous tension between the Kingdom of God he announced and wealth. Money and wealth, far from being neutral in their effect on people, could easily cause them to serve the wrong God: 'No one can be a slave of two masters; he will hate one and love the other; he will be loyal to one and despise the other. You cannot serve both God and money' (Matthew 6:24).

Jesus announced that the qualities of love and justice come together in such a way as to be good news for the poor. There are many references to this in the Gospels. For instance, we see that charitable giving always comes a poor second behind justice. Jesus expected that the values of generosity and personal giving would be found in the wealthy, even to the extent of selling all their possessions (Luke 12:33). Free, generous, discreet (and often anonymous) giving removes the existence of a condescending 'looking down on' stance on the part of the donor, replacing it with neighbourliness and respect. In fact, the debate around poverty often overlooks the fact that Jesus focused equally on wealth. This presents a significant challenge to our consumer society, which is preoccupied with self-accumulation and characterised by greed and personal gain. While it is true that Jesus' ministry was directed towards the poor, his focus on money and wealth constituted a significant part of his teaching – he spoke more about money than he did about Heaven.

The issue of poverty may not be the main focus when considering the poor. More important is the issue of wealth and how we use it. As Gamble writes: 'The question to be asked is not what we should give to the poor but what will we stop taking from the poor. The poor are not our problem, we are their problem!'[4]

The attitude of the wealthy towards the poor is a dominant theme in Jesus' teaching. The rich young man who wanted to know what he had to do to get eternal life did not go away sad because he was rich. He went away sad because his values were wrong. It was his inability to give up his wealth, at Jesus' command, that excluded him from following Christ. In giving to the poor, we give to Christ, and demonstrate that our treasure is indeed where it ought to be – laid up in Heaven (Matthew 6:20-21).

In the light of this teaching we understand that The Salvation Army is not a church *for* the poor, it is a church *with* the poor and, to some degree, *of* the poor. We can work at solving the problem of poverty collaboratively.

From the teaching of Jesus, we obtain a Kingdom perspective on the relationship of the gospel to the poor. As The Salvation Army we affirm our commitment to serving suffering humanity as a response to and reflection of the ministry of Jesus to the poor.

Evangelism and social action

Questions concerning the relationship between evangelism and social action have intrigued biblical scholars for much of the past 150 years. Some place a total emphasis on evangelism to the exclusion of social action altogether, while others veer towards a 'social gospel' which minimises the requirement for evangelism (or indeed any form of orthodox Christian spirituality), with Jesus becoming the benevolent sympathiser rather than the crucified Saviour.

Then there are those who acknowledge the need for both, but declare that evangelism must always take precedence. After all, they argue, if we were successful in evangelising the whole world, the social issues would take care of themselves. However, such an argument assumes that evangelism is always necessarily the starting point for mission. Even if this were desirable, it is not always possible. The well known incident of William Booth passing homeless and hungry people while walking along London's Embankment and over Blackfriars Bridge resulted in him telling his son Bramwell to 'go and do something' about their plight. It was apparent to them both that there was no point in preaching to a person's soul while his or her stomach was empty.

It is the immediate, presenting need of people that must be responded to as part of the mission. To think otherwise would not resonate with the life and ministry of Jesus. The starting point in his interactions with people varied from physically healing them to forming friendships (for example, going for a meal with Zacchaeus at his house in Luke 19). Jesus always started with a person's immediate need and developed the relationship from that point. What can be said is that, wherever the relationship started, almost always it graduated to the things of God and spiritual healing and wholeness.

While evangelism can be said to deal with a person's ultimate need and destiny in terms of his or her salvation, social action is a missional response to the presenting need, which communicates hope to the individual that his or her situation can be transformed.

Overall, however, the issue of where we start the mission is not the chief concern. The main thing is that we respond with an awareness of both the immediate and the ultimate needs. Admittedly, the relationship between the two is complex, but the Army must ensure that the balance is always struck in the delivery of its front-line programmes. Plentiful evidence of this holistic approach can be found in the very presence of Salvation Army schools, hostels, hospitals, community programmes and, of course, churches in so many countries around the world.

Not to present our mission in this holistic manner is to fail in God's requirement of us as his people. We would fail to align our 'mission model' alongside that which we see clearly demonstrated by Jesus.

Strategic focus
The implication for Salvation Army Social Services (SASS) in its ministry to serve suffering humanity is to embrace the concept that the whole of the Church needs to respond to the challenge of the whole of the mission of God towards humankind. This mission cannot be accomplished in isolation. The challenge is to present holistic mission in our centres, corps and other units (such as Red Shield centres, older people's homes, prisons etc). This remains the strategic focus of the entire organisation.

The challenge in organisational terms is that, for a variety of reasons, there is a functional separation between the evangelism and the social service dimensions. The root of this is partly historical in that SASS operated for many years as a separate administrative and operational dimension of The Salvation Army in the UK, with its own headquarters structures and systems. In recent years SASS has been brought together with evangelism under the banner of 'Programme

Service' at a high level in the organisation. However, a perception remains that a 'distance' is retained both in terms of operational functionality and evangelism strategy (although the Territorial Social Services Strategy Council was formed to address this).

This contrived separation may still be necessary for two main reasons. First, the complexity of funding arrangements for SASS has significant legal implications for The Salvation Army Trustee Company. Funding for SASS is multi-sourced – for example, from government, trusts and partnerships with local authorities and commercial enterprises. It is important to keep this separate from church-based work, which aspires, quite rightly, to be funded by its members. The second reason is the very specific skill sets and qualifications required for social service staff. The demand for careful compliance in this area necessitates a highly specialised management and resource system to support it. This is increasingly the case as social services in the UK become more and more professional – and legally accountable, both internally and externally. It is good to affirm that, at this juncture in our history, SASS has never had such a high level of professionalism in its practice.

However, the challenge is whether the effectiveness of the evangelism mandate matches the excellence of the social action mandate.

Presently, evangelism in SASS is largely dependent on chaplaincy. Historically the evangelism mandate rested fully with the officers responsible for the operations of a centre and the spiritual impact this had on residents. There are still some Salvation Army officers managing SASS centres (as well as managers who are Christians), and they seek to work from a well-balanced social service and evangelism mandate. However, because they are relatively few, we cannot rely on their presence alone to implement an effective evangelism strategy in SASS.

It is possible that the demand for professionalism in this service may be diminishing the evangelism function. But we should not automatically assume that a more holistic and balanced approach is no longer possible.

Integrated mission

Asking the right questions will better enable us to balance our dual mission mandate of immediacy and ultimacy (social action and evangelism). This in turn will lead us in the direction of more integrated mission. It will also ensure that we are united, strategically and practically, in our evangelism mandate, while acknowledging that some partition may be necessary for purposes of administration and operation.

I believe the most pressing need is to develop further a broad, innovative national evangelism strategy within SASS. This could be aligned to the international Salvation Army initiative Health, Healing and Wholeness, instigated at International Headquarters and embraced by the UK Territory (see Appendix 1). Concerning the evangelism mandate, item 10 states:

> 'Salvation through Jesus Christ is central to the Army's purpose and provides transforming power in all its ministries. For this reason, evangelism and discipling contribute to health, healing and wholeness.'

A national strategy should not be prescriptive, but should provide a balanced, robust framework for the development of the spiritual programme in SASS centres. We need to create opportunities to share our faith and proclaim the gospel appropriately in this context sensitively and wisely. We also need to support and resource managers in this vital mission area. One way forward in these areas is to create more effective bridges between social service centres and Salvation Army corps (churches), reflecting the reality that the missionary task should involve the whole of the church. Many of our corps are within easy access of SASS centres.

If the principle is accepted that the missionary task of The Salvation Army should involve the whole church, then it may make sense to set up at every social service centre a Mission Focus Group. This group's purpose would be to develop, plan and monitor the evangelism strategy in the centre, ensuring the corps and centre co-ordinated and 'meshed' their respective mission strategies. Members of the group could include centre manager and deputy, chaplain, some staff members and residents, the local corps officers (remembering there may be more than one), a couple of local officers (ideally recruiting sergeant and corps sergeant-major), along with divisional directors of evangelism and social services.

For residents coming to faith, it is imperative that strong links are made with a church – ideally a Salvation Army corps – so that the new disciple becomes part of the body of Christ. The excellent research contained in *The Seeds of Exclusion*, a report published by The Salvation Army in 2008, points us towards a more integrated approach to supporting clients in our centres and ensuring they have the opportunity to develop networks in the community that can be developed beyond their tenure in the centre[5]. Our corps have a great capacity for community cohesion and, with imagination, our community programmes could dovetail with work being carried out in centres. As a result of this report some excellent work has been done with trying to benchmark corps community programmes in terms of their missionary effectiveness. This concept contains the potential to transform our approach to our community work.

Is there an opportunity to integrate the centre's project workers' tasks with the community programme in the corps? For example, many corps are looking at integrating Employment Plus (finding work for the unemployed) into their programmes, and this aspect would certainly benefit residents.

Corps also need to develop a greater understanding of the specific spiritual needs of residents. In New Zealand the concept of Recovery Churches (for people with issues of addiction and abuse) has gained momentum and has much to commend it. This concept acknowledges the particular needs of the client group, while understanding that connection to the local corps will provide enormous advantages. There is a tension here between the needs of the clients as a specific group and the need for them to belong to and be supported by a Christian community whose culture may be many steps removed from theirs. The question arises: 'Should we be developing a homogenous church for people with these issues?' Such a fellowship would be designed with the client group in mind, rather than expecting them to adapt themselves to the way a particular corps worships.

If our corps can provide fellowship and support for people according to their age or gender, leisure or musical interest, surely they could also provide support, worship and fellowship opportunities for residents and other people who are recovering from a variety of addictions and behaviours.

Corps need to provide opportunities for clients to work as volunteers and find appropriate, useful roles in the community programme, for example as café volunteers or in maintenance roles.

The challenge for corps
Having considered the challenge of the SASS programme and its evangelism mandate, we also need to challenge our corps-based mission about its social service mandate. A corps with no expression of social service or community engagement presents an equally flawed picture.

Society places an emphasis on 'social capital', which is fundamentally about building bridges with people who do not belong and connecting them. Society also values 'social cohesion' which is about building trust between groupings in our communities. This goes beyond a donor-orientated 'we give and you take' exercise. This new opportunity calls for engagement between the Army and its communities, implying long-term commitment, in-depth knowledge and practical pastoral care.

Theologian Ann Morisy writes:

> 'The availability of churches and church halls for use by the wider community is one of the taken-for-granted aspects of British life... [It is] one of the underestimated contributions by churches to social capital and social cohesion in many communities. Churches have proved more successful than local authorities and tenants and residents' groups at running and maintaining facilities for community groups. However, what churches have been less successful at is tracking and articulating how this open and often generous access translates into mission.'[6]

We could create the spaces and the environments for 'community capital' to be built, where people who have never spoken to one another converse and build relationships and trust.

Some of the traditional groups in our community programmes would be ideal for this approach. Parent-and-toddler sessions and lunch clubs come readily to mind as presenting opportunities to bring together people from different cultural, ethnic, racial and religious backgrounds.

In conclusion, it may be that our own structures are less than ideal in allowing The Salvation Army to balance its dual mission. If that is the reality, the onus rests both on leaders and every one of us to discover innovative ways to ensure that due priority is placed on both mission mandates – and in particular to facilitate and resource the ultimate aim of all Salvation Army work, to bring people into a saving knowledge of Jesus Christ.

CHAPTER SEVEN

Moving Forward

'So [Jesus] replied, "This means, then, that every teacher of the Law who becomes a disciple in the Kingdom of heaven is like the owner of a house who takes new and old things out of his storage room"' (Matthew 13:52).

SPIRITUAL renewal in The Salvation Army will, in all likelihood, manifest itself in a manner that allows the three dominant charisms we have looked at to flourish as our Movement reconnects to the mission of God. The beneficiaries of this renewal will be those to whom the mission is directed. If God's people are to experience his renewing presence, it will be for the purpose of energising them for his mission, enabling them to become agents of transformation in society as Jesus is incarnated through their lives.

There are alternatives to renewal of course. We could choose to 'bury our heads in the sand' or 'fiddle while Rome burns' and hope that it will all turn out all right. We may think that we can escape, get out alive and without blame by adopting a position where we resist the challenge of renewal. However, the consequences of our doing so do not bear thinking about. Chapters two and three of the final book of the Bible, the Revelation of John, are worth reading and digesting as examples of churches that lost their way in the service of God. The instruction given to those churches was that they both take heed of the diagnosis of their condition and receive the corrective prescription offered. We go from the loss of 'first love' in the church at Ephesus, with its outwardly correct forms and worship – which George Campbell Morgan accurately describes as 'faultily faultless, and flawlessly flawed' – to the lukewarm Laodicean church which made God sick by its indifference. Apart from the one written to Laodicea, the letters to the churches in Revelation all contain a recipe for renewal, revealing the longing of Jesus for his Bride, the Church, to be at his side, engaged in her calling to make disciples of all nations.

United Kingdom Territory officer Major Phillip Escott's extrapolation of statistical trends, which he prepared in the early 1990s as part of the 20/20 Vision initiative, predicted that without intervention The Salvation Army in the UK would not be a viable entity by the year 2020. This forecast, while appearing gloomy and alarmist, was set in the context of an optimistic expectation. Underlying the desire that people ought to face the brutal facts was a passionately held belief that the Holy Spirit would intervene with renewal and revival. The expectation was that The Salvation Army would respond to the fresh wind of God's presence and grace. I think most Salvationists would agree that we want to leave a legacy of a more effective mission-driven Salvation Army than the one we joined, and so we welcome and embrace the promptings of the Holy Spirit.

It seems clear that the dangers of spiritual fervency cooling into tepid irrelevance and losing the first love are very real threats to any Christian church. So, with holy fear we implore the Holy Spirit to renew this Movement and fit it for God's mission.

Perpetual challenge

However, there is a perpetual challenge facing faith communities as they prepare to move forward: that of working out how to reach people in today's largely consumer culture with the gospel message. This might result in people having to move out of their preferred spheres of worship and service – and William Booth was adept at encouraging people to do that. As *Mission-Shaped Church*, a report from the Church of England says:

> 'Holiness as separation for God's purposes leads to the call to a distinctively holy life. At the heart of such holiness is the willingness to die to one's own comfort and preferences and be made alive to God's. It is a holy church that is willing to die to its own culture in order to live for God in another.'[1]

Bible history tells us that the people of God never stand still. Whether it is escaping the flood in an ark, trudging through a wilderness for 40 years, or moving forward to a promised land, you could not say that God's people were exactly settled.

When people receive Christ they begin a faith journey that transforms them. Faith calls them to grow and develop and become more like Christ. As they journey, keeping the cross at the centre of their lives, they face the challenge of overcoming their fears and resistance and responding in faith to God's calling on their lives. The challenge may be to specific areas of obedience – for example, lifestyle, personal ambition or a relationship. As they respond in obedience to the Holy Spirit their life in Christ enlarges and they grow in their faith. This will happen again and again as they undertake this journey. Christians present themselves to Christ every day as 'a living sacrifice, holy and acceptable to God' (Romans 12:1).

What is true about the journey of an individual will be true for the journey of any church or Christian community. When we pray to retrieve the charisms and seek spiritual renewal and mission effectiveness, we immediately realise that obedience and faith are required. This will undoubtedly mean that we as individuals and as a denomination will be driven out of our comfort zones and will experience the cost as we journey forward. Fear will be a factor here – fear of losing something (such as our identity), fear of change itself and fear of failure. However, we take heart because we are a resurrection and Pentecost people! We, like our Lord Jesus, endure the cross because of the hope that has been set before us (Hebrews 12:2).

Liminality

Liminality is an anthropological term that applies to people who are at an in-between stage. This is a place where there could be danger and risk, a place where breakthrough occurs and growth and renewal happen where they would not have otherwise. It could be said that The Salvation Army is in such a place.

In *The Forgotten* Ways Alan Hirsch refers to studies of tribes in places such as Africa, where young boys live with their mothers until they are around 12 years of age[2]. At the appropriate time the men in the village take the boys away from their mothers and relocate them, as a small group, in the bush. They are often circumcised at this point and then left to fend for themselves in the wild for anything up to six months. Once a month the head men visit to debrief and mentor them. But on the whole the boys have to find the resources in themselves to cope and survive. As a group they frequently bond into a strong community. They emerge from those experiences having learnt a great deal and re-enter their village, no longer as boys but as adult men.

Examples of the liminality concept in Scripture are numerous. For example, Abraham was not a settler but a pilgrim who held to a vision that God had given him. Look at the verbs used in Genesis chapters 12 and 13 alone which describe his travels: 'started out' (12:4), 'arrived' (12:5), 'travelled through' (12:6), 'moved on south' (12:8), 'moved on' (12:9), 'went farther south' (12:10), 'went north out of' (13:1), 'left there' (13:3), 'moved from place to place' (13:3), 'moved his camp' (13:18).

F. B. Meyer, in his book *Abraham*, implies that liminality was a frequent experience for this patriarch, one he learnt to welcome[3]. Abraham's pattern was to pitch his tent and build an altar at every place he stopped (see Genesis 12 and 13).

The tent, says Meyer, represents the temporary status of our present life with its material accumulations, hollow achievements and human ambitions. Abraham had them but held them lightly. When God said 'Go', he packed up and moved on in obedient faith. The tent had no foundations that may have prevented him responding immediately to God's call. It was a constant reminder of the temporary nature of the things of this earth, and of the detachment required if we are to see ourselves as disciples, as 'living sacrifices' (Romans 12:1).

In each place he stopped, Abraham built an altar of 12 stones. If someone happened to arrive at his campsite at some future point they would not find remnants of the tent but the altar, which would be still visible. The memory that remained was that a man of God had been in that place. Abraham's memorial was his altars. His significant milestones were not educational or business achievements, wealth or status gained, but altars where great sacrifices were made so that God's will could be accomplished in his life. Liminality was a part of his lifestyle.

New Testament examples of liminality include Paul, whose life was marked by whippings, beatings, shipwrecks and stonings. His journey was anything but secure and comfortable. Then there is John on the island of Patmos and Peter, who became 'the rock'.

The greatest example of liminality, however, is Jesus, leaving the splendour and glory of Heaven and coming to earth with not even a place to lay his head. He called his disciples to leave everything and follow him. He did not prepare them for the calling in the classroom of an academy but on the road in the dangerous conditions of a Roman-occupied land, while all the time dealing with the scheming and corrupt leaders of the Jewish religious system.

To overcome the comfort and convenience of the 'huddle-and-cuddle' Church of the modern era, the Holy Spirit may call us to embark on a dangerous journey – to shake off our securities and discover that mission drives us out into a world of action where disciples might experience disorientation, vulnerability and marginalisation. Nevertheless, as history proves, this is the way that we encounter God – and one another – in new and exciting ways. If we are going to become effective in mission this may be our path to renewal. It will involve adventure, movement and a new togetherness (*koinonia*).

The Salvation Army

The Salvation Army in the UK has become a diverse church, with diverse expressions of its mission. There are large citadels with all the 'trimmings', and small corps without them. We can find 614 networks – formerly NEOs (new expressions of) – and their almost unrecognisable and 'messy' Salvation Army mission. Retrieving the charisms explored in this book and discovering spiritual renewal will unite us all in the mission of God.

It is disappointing when people in Army settings criticise others whose work and worship is different from their own – surely there is room for everyone. The words 'either/or' need to be replaced by 'and' in our vocabulary. To imagine that any Salvation Army expression will become fixed and rigid is to deny the very pragmatism that brought us into existence. It is inconceivable that the God who created a universe full of different stars and galaxies, and who made a human race where no two faces or fingerprints are identical, would want a Church of monochrome personality, music taste, gifting or opinion.

Retrieving the charisms of soul-saving, holiness and serving suffering humanity will impact inherited Salvation Army corps and new expressions of The Salvation Army, both of which are vitally needed if we are to reach into our culture with the gospel.

It is imperative that the inherited Army be open to spiritual renewal and to retrieving the charisms as it develops its life under God. It needs to do this in order to retain its healthiness. An unhealthy church cannot or will not grow.

Every corps needs to recognise the danger of adopting a merely preservationist mentality and resisting any attempt to introduce intelligent, Holy Spirit-led change. Such an attitude will lead to that corps becoming a cultural capsule of irrelevance in its community. General Bramwell Tillsley in *The Officer* magazine tracked how a movement can become a museum:

> 'In the first stage, it might be described as a "Movement". Here "advance" is the war cry. The adherents of such movements are marked by intensity, fervency and zeal. The consciousness of divine leadership is strong. The moving of the Spirit is central...'

He goes on to explain that in the second stage the movement stabilises and becomes an institution. The final stage, he says:

> '... is when the "institution" becomes a "museum". Here, devotees gather to worship the past and speak of bygone days. They may still have the reputation of being alive, but in reality are dead... Is it possible that we have entered stage two, having regressed from a "movement" to an "institution"?'[4]

If we are committed to being an alive expression of Church, it is essential that the inherited Army constantly renews its intention to be a missionary movement. This will probably mean we will be in a continuing state of transition. However, our mission is not only defined by what we do, it is also defined by what we do not do. Commissioner Phil Needham makes this point well in his book *Community In Mission*:

> 'We must seek to understand what are the roots and what are the branches in Church tradition. We must know what can be discarded (pruned) and what must remain.'[5]

The commissioner argues that roots which provide the stability for growth are more important than branches that need to be pruned. He encourages us to decide what to take on our journey and to shed the extraneous baggage, leaving it behind as it just slows us down and paralyses us.

Corps need to spend time reflecting on the critical areas of mission. The NEWS (**N**urture, **E**vangelism, **W**orship, **S**ervice) acrostic, based on Acts 2:42-47, is a simple but nonetheless helpful concept which may help us to think about the key purposes of a missionary church in the world. The outline develops as follows:

Nurture

We have already discussed the need, in an increasingly post-Christendom context, to develop disciples carefully. The less people know about Christianity and the story of Jesus when they join us, the more they need to be taught. After all, Jesus needed three years to teach and train his disciples – and they had a head start. They at least knew the story because of their Jewish roots. Discipleship is not something to be rushed just for the sake of getting people actively involved and signed up.

Evangelism

The challenge for the inherited corps is to reflect on whether its present method of proclaiming the gospel is the best one, and what other options are open to it. Every corps needs a deliberate, carefully thought out strategy for telling the story.

The arrival on the scene of courses such as Alpha, Emmaus, Christianity Explored and Discipleship Explored have been a gift to the Church and many of our corps are quite rightly incorporating these into their programmes on a regular basis. Telling the story in school assemblies is another ripe opportunity as is our work in prisons and Red Shield centres.

Small groups provide an opportunity for mission-shaped evangelism. The cell church relies solely on the concept that church *is* the small group, and that the group grows and replicates itself constantly as new members are saved, discipled and added to the 'church' or 'cell'. While not every church is, or will be, a cell church, the model offers the inherited church something that it probably cannot grow without.

We referred earlier to open-air meetings which many corps still pursue with admirable commitment. There are a number of ways to make this ministry as effective as possible.

For example, corps could produce a small number of captivating open-air services that are fast moving, attention grabbing and visual, which can be repeated in a loop. These could feature well-prepared short, sharp testimonies, presented by both uniformed and non-uniformed people of both genders and various ages. There could be more variety in the music used and a few carefully prepared drama presentations. This involves work and commitment, and corps may need to consider running workshops instead of open-air meetings for a few weeks each year in order to prepare creatively and thoroughly.

Corps could train people in one-to-one evangelism so open-air ministry is backed up with good conversations. There are excellent training resources on the market, such as *Just Walk across the Room* and *Becoming a Contagious Christian* from Willow Creek Church. Also, well produced literature is always effective.

However, people not only need to be trained to share their faith in corps-based initiatives, but in their weekday networks as well. The role of the corps must be to equip people for whole-of-life mission. As the congregation disperses on Sunday they are entering the arena of mission and faith-sharing and they need to be resourced for this task.

Another group that will benefit from receiving training and support is those involved with running the weekday community programme. Thousands of people enter many of our halls each week – how well prepared are we to share Christ with them?

Worship
The primary purpose of regularly meeting together is to worship God. The writer of Hebrews tell us not to neglect meeting together

for this very purpose (Hebrews 10:25). When people truly worship there is one Person in the audience – God and God alone. He is 'the only proper object of religious worship', as our doctrines remind us. We do not own worship. Having said that, any act of worship contains within it a potential to raise an awareness of the presence of God in those who have gathered together. The vital challenge for the inherited corps is to understand exactly who the worship is designed for. Is it designed for us, catering for our preferences, traditions and our tastes in music? Or is it designed for others, that is, those who do not regularly attend and who have no personal faith in Christ?

We need to think about the needs of the unbeliever when we prepare any act of worship. Here are some important considerations: the worship almost certainly will need to be more informal and relaxed in its presentation style, without sacrificing the substance, content, beauty or depth of the worship experience. The music needs to be the best it can be – in many inherited corps there are fine brass and contemporary groups which can complement each other. The preaching needs to be inspiring, relevant and biblically founded.

Service to the body
A great challenge for the inherited corps will hinge on its understanding of leadership. The model of ministry in the New Testament is one where the whole Church engages itself in the whole mission and the whole ministry of the Church. The modern Church model is one where people go to the church/corps to be ministered to by a paid, ordained, professional minister/officer. Consequently, a clash of expectations can arise between the leader giving the ministry and the congregation receiving it. The congregation place (often unspoken) expectations on the officer, who may respond by trying to 'perform' ministry in order to satisfy his or her flock. This results in the disempowering of the local congregation and often the burn-out of the leader. One way

to address this is for officers and paid leaders to 'give away' the ministry of the corps to the congregation and see their role, as St Paul expressed it, in terms of preparing:

> '... all God's people for the work of Christian service, in order to build up the body of Christ. And so we shall all come together to that oneness in our faith and in our knowledge of the Son of God; we shall become mature people, reaching to the very height of Christ's full stature' (Ephesians 4:12-14).

The role of officers is to facilitate, stimulate and resource people to be ministers. General John Gowans once spoke to a congregation at a national congress, inviting all the ministers to stand. All the officers stood up while the rest of the congregation remained seated. The General repeated his invitation with no further impact on the scene. He then explained that all Salvationists should see themselves as ministers. He wanted everyone on their feet – or more importantly, involved in ministry.

Hirsch's *The Forgotten Ways*, which I have referred to a number of times, is actually based on the study of the Chinese Church which was forced underground during the reign of Mao Tse-tung. Mao attempted to purge China of the Christian faith, closing churches and confiscating property, banning clergy and expelling all foreign missionaries. All Christian gatherings were outlawed with threat of torture and even death. The aim was to obliterate the Christian religion. What actually happened was that the two million or so Chinese Christians who were forced underground flourished beyond imagination. When the ban was lifted it is estimated that between 60 and 80 million Christians emerged! Some suggest that this may be the most significant transformational movement in the history of the Church. It was done with no professional clergy, denominational structures, mass meetings or congresses and no money was poured into it.

Spiritual renewal does not just involve full-time officer leaders, but all of us. The full-time leader is there to lead the leaders, to facilitate the mission, to work in and with a team of people who are in that place for the long haul.

Leadership expert Jim Collins, in his book *Good To Great*, gives a helpful analogy of a bus journey:

> 'Look, I don't really know where we should take this bus. But I know this much: if we get the right people on the bus, the right people in the right seats, and the wrong people off the bus, then we'll figure out how to take it someplace great.'[6]

The leader, says Collins, does not make the mistake of thinking that he or she must possess or generate all the vision. Instead, the leader gets the right people on the bus, in the right seats, and understands that they will take the bus to its destination.

Salvation Army tradition and policy insists that the officer is the 'commanding officer'[7]. This is healthy, so long as the leader understands that a key leadership skill is to select and lead the right team. There are people in every corps who have influence and who are respected. When they move in a direction, they take others in the fellowship with them. The leader's priority is to get the right team in place, and then resource that team to lead a missionary people.

There is a rich mix of spiritual gifts, unique life experiences, natural talents, varied temperaments and individual faith journeys in our congregations. William Booth referred to this as 'buried treasure'. All of it must be valued and given expression both in and beyond the life of the corps. The truly missionary congregation will be the one that deliberately resources and enables its people to engage in a whole-of-life ministry, rather than in the corps/church's concerns and agendas.

We need to legitimise and discover ways by which we can affirm our people as they engage in mission in their neighbourhoods, schools, universities and workplaces. Martyn Atkins puts it beautifully: 'A "new laity" is emerging that requires a "new clergy", who together form a "new ministry", an inclusive partnership appropriate for a challenging mission context and consequently embodying a greater possibility of renewal.'[8]

The Salvation Army has a tradition of giving strong emphasis to children's and youth ministry. However, this ambition is not reflected in the age profile of most of our corps. We are not a young Army. This requires urgent attention because, as we grow older, we become less able to engage effectively with children and young people. It is clear that they need to be engaged in owning the church and its future. We need to give our church away to the young!

Attractive corps provide facilities and programmes for children and young people. These are the corps that understand what Jesus meant when he placed a child at the centre of the group of disciples and stated that this represented the Kingdom of God (see Matthew 18:1-6). Jesus also gave a warning about the consequences for those who prevent children from reaching him. Churches that make children feel valued, safe and welcome, with all their unpredictable noise and chaos, demonstrate Kingdom of God principles and culture.

In a survey of churches conducted by the Methodist Church, it was found that large churches are doing particularly well in Britain today, the main reason being that they provide facilities for children and youth[9]. Ministry in schools, as has already been mentioned, is a wide-open door at the moment and it would be wise to invest in training and resourcing to maximise this opportunity. The Salvation Army in the UK has developed resource packs for children in schools.

Service to the community
Effective community outreach in our corps/centres has been one of The Salvation Army's historical strengths. The justifiable pride with which many Salvationists speak when they remember goodwill centres and the teams that worked tirelessly with the poor is but

one evidence of this legacy. Community service will increasingly involve working in partnership with local authorities and other community groups and networks, as well as other churches. Matching the strengths and gifting found in a congregation to the many opportunities for ministry and mission in the community is a key task for local Army leadership.

It is inconceivable that a Salvation Army corps should not be engaged within its community. The community is the mission field. 'Who is my neighbour?' is primarily a question of context and mission. 'Whom do we serve?' is another way of stating this question. The Alban Institute's Alice Mann quotes author Ed White, who poses a number of key questions:

> 'Is your congregation primarily in the fellowship business?
> 'Is your congregation primarily in the business of calling people into discipleship and forming them in a life-changing faith?'[10]

Mann adds her own questions to this list:

> 'Is your congregation primarily in the music business?
> 'Is your congregation primarily in the historic preservation business?
> 'Is your congregation primarily in the landlord business?
> 'Is your congregation primarily in the investment management business?'[11]

If the answer to the primary question as to whom we serve is 'our own people', then I concur with William Booth – we should close the doors and die a dignified death. His passion was for 'others'.

However, there are other options.

The report *The Seeds of Exclusion* began as a telephone survey of corps with community service programmes, ranking the effectiveness of these in five different levels (see Appendix Two). The four areas examined were worship and pastoral care; community-focused work/support groups; partnership with external organisations; and mission reflecting community needs, including supporting children and families, people in transition and vulnerable people and speaking out for marginalised people.

This research provides a conceptual framework by which a corps can assess its community service and outreach. Having benchmarked its position, the corps can then develop a strategy that takes it towards the desired Level 5. In fact, this could be further simplified and made even more 'user-friendly'. I would also suggest the addition of the discipleship concept 'Key Stage One', which challenges a corps to consider the strategy it has in place for inviting people who use the community programme to hear about the gospel of Jesus (see Appendix Three). Intentional links should be created in groups such as parent-and-toddler groups and luncheon clubs, so options are available which encourage them to hear the gospel story. Examples of such links could be Babysong, Alpha courses, corps social events, family services and house groups.

Also important is the need to think differently and strategically as funding for community programmes is being devolved more and more to local authorities. The involvement of Christians in community planning committees is vital. Very few Christians occupy the Third Sector or interfaith seats on these groups, and if we fail to respond to this challenge we will miss a huge opportunity.

To sum up, developing a vision of an effective, vibrant, missionary Salvation Army corps or centre is immensely exciting. It removes the depressing prospect that what we are experiencing at present is inevitable and replaces it with the ability to see what God wants to see. It inspires faith and hope. It attracts new generations of young people to give their lives to its realisation. The UK Salvation Army Vision Statement was devised by a group of people with an average age of 35 years. It continues to inspire:

'As disciples of Jesus Christ, we will be a Spirit-filled, radical, growing movement with a burning desire to lead people into a saving knowledge of Jesus Christ, actively serve the community, and fight for social justice.'

Conclusion

'The Church of Jesus Christ is yet to be.
May our memories not be a barrier to our imagination.'[1]

Peter Neilsen

WHAT place does the past have in the future? We have looked at how our recollection of the founding visions might shape the future Army and how our memories of the Salvation Army story could give us a clue as to what God wants to do with us in the 21st century. However, there is a danger of becoming paralysed by what we recollect, of being stuck in a time warp. Alternatively, our collective historical memory of the Army's story could enable us to break out of our preferred areas of service and imagine a future Army engaged in God's mission in the world – if we allowed it to. These are some of the themes that have occupied our thinking in the pages of this book.

I stated in the introduction that this book is born out of these two important, inextricably linked themes – mission and spiritual renewal. I set out to demonstrate that without spiritual renewal, mission will atrophy and die over time. And without mission, spiritual renewal is a self-centred indulgence that will not impact our world or society.

There is little doubt that our founders were able to read the signs of their times and to incarnate the gospel in such a way that people were compelled to respond to the very presence of Christ

91

among them. Incarnational mission it certainly was. It was also a prophetic expression of the good news, in that it involved not only being anointed to read the signs of times, but also speaking God's word into that context in a way that brought a fresh expression of God's Kingdom in the midst of it. In The Salvation Army we are a little shy of declaring that our ministry, message and mission are prophetic – but that it is precisely what they need to be.

Developing our ability to read the signs of the times and to speak God's word (good news) into our complex and multifaceted society is a demanding challenge. However, it is precisely what God is calling us to do, and he promises through the Holy Spirit to equip us for the task. It is for this reason that I wanted to write this book. I wanted to articulate the hope that as God continues to 'reconcile all things to himself' the Army will be spiritually renewed as it embraces and engages with his mission.

We have a bigger purpose than to merely exist. God help us if we see denominational survival alone as a worthy ambition! The bigger purpose is that:

> '...in honour of the name of Jesus all beings in heaven, on earth, and in the world below will fall on their knees, and all will openly proclaim that Jesus Christ is Lord, to the glory of God the Father' (Philippians 2:10-11).

The bigger purpose is: 'May your Kingdom come; may your will be done on earth as it is in heaven' (Matthew 6:10). The bigger purpose is: 'For God loved the world so much...' (John 3:16). If we exist for anything less or anything other than the bigger purpose then I suspect we will find ourselves in the same place as the Laodicean church in Revelation 3:14ff, where Christ, excluded from that inward-focused and self-absorbed church, is seen knocking on the door, pleading for someone to hear his missionary call.

Jim Collins entitled Chapter 4 of his book *Good to Great*: 'Confront the Brutal Facts (Yet Never Lose Faith)'[2] – and we need to heed that advice. Hope and faith are challenged by 'facts', among which are declining attendances, the increased marginalisation of the Church in society, widespread indifference, and a generally held view that personal faith can be tolerated as long as it is kept private. The fact is The Salvation Army in the UK is an older, smaller Army in these early 21st-century decades than it was as it moved out of the 19th century. General William Booth spoke of 'the good time coming'[3] as the Army entered the new millennium at the dawn of the 20th century. Could we say the same thing as we start to journey through the 21st century?

I would say yes, we can! Since when did 'facts' determine our faith? We see, with the eye of faith, that God is at work in the world. 'God [*still*] so loves the world' (John 3:16) and is reconciling everything to himself: 'God was in Christ reconciling the world unto himself' (2 Corinthians 5:19 *ASV*).

And I suggest this can happen as we claim once again the charisms of saving souls, holiness and serving suffering humanity – gifts which fulfil Christ's purpose and mission in the world and which are for the good of others.

God is still moving towards 'thy Kingdom come'. And what is more, he is with us as we move forward in mission with him. The Salvation Army refuses to be paralysed by the fear and uncertainty that the 'facts' suggest are apt in such times. We advance intrepidly with the same hope that General Booth expressed, of 'the good time coming'. Nothing will convince me otherwise as we commit ourselves to the mission of God. His presence is all that we need. The Holy Spirit will renew our hearts as we engage in mission with him, anticipating and expecting that our communities will be transformed by the living presence of Jesus Christ.

As much as I love being blessed by God in the deep places of my own soul, I declare that this alone cannot ever be sufficient. If that is all that spiritual renewal entails, then it is not for me. What I long for is a personal renewal that will allow God to breathe his life through me into people who don't yet know him. If the renewing of this heart of mine is the means through which that can happen, then I want nothing more than the Holy Spirit's continuous anointing on my life. As Lieut-Colonel Colin Fairclough's song (*SASB* 479) says:

'That the world may ever see
Christ, and only Christ, in me.'

Notes on Chapters

Chapter One

[1] Quoted in Atkins M., *Resourcing Renewal* (Peterborough: Inspire, 2007), p245

[2] Allen R., *Missionary Methods, St Paul's or Ours* (Grand Rapids: Erdmans Printing Company, 1962), p3

[3] Bosch D., *Transforming Mission* (New York: Orbis Books, 1991), p380

[4] Gibbs E., *Followed or Pushed?* (Bromley: MARC Europe, 1987), p55

[5] Sweet L., *Soul Tsunami* (Grand Rapids: Zondervan Publishing House, 1999), p89. By 'futurist' I mean a visionary who challenges the Church about its mission.

[6] Uniform-wearing: By this I mean formal uniform with tunics, hats/caps, etc. Many liberal Salvationists value uniform, but a more modern, less formal 'logo-identifying' dress code. For example, many students are now wearing T-shirts, 'hoodies' or polo shirts with a red shield or other type of Salvation Army logo around their university campuses or when they hang out with their friends. This could be said to align to the original purpose of uniform for witness, where the early Salvationists would wear their uniforms to work etc, rather than keeping them as a 'Sunday outfit' for church.

[7] ALOVE Mission Statement: 'ALOVE UK is The Salvation Army for a new generation. Our mission is to call a generation to dynamic faith, radical lifestyles, adventurous mission and to fight for justice.'

[8] Mann A., *Can our Church Live?* (USA: The Alban Institute, 1999, reprinted 2000), p1

Chapter Two

[1] Romano A., *The Charism of the Founders* (Maynooth: St Paul's, 1989), p73

[2] Donnelly D., *Retrieving the Charisms for the 21st Century* (Collegeville: The Liturgical Press, 1999), p12

[3] The founder is the name given to the person who initiates a movement or organisation and thus establishes the principles and values on which it proceeds. Those who join the movement identify with, and often receive for themselves, the same charism or mix of charisms.

[4] Donnelly (1999), p141

[5] ibid p24

[6] ibid p5

[7] Saarinen M., *Special Paper and Research Report, The Life Cycle of a Congregation* (Bethesda: The Alban Institute, 1986), p12

[8] Hattersley R., *Blood and Fire: William and Catherine Booth and The Salvation Army* (London: Abacus, 2000), p9

[9] Donnelly (1999), px

[10] ROOTS exists to call Salvationists to biblical Christianity, radical discipleship, contemporary communication of the gospel and a passion for the lost, which are at the 'root' of The Salvation Army and the Christian Church. ROOTS is therefore committed to and characterised by the following core values:

- The powerful, present, indwelling reality of the Holy Spirit and his sanctification, transforming us as disciples into the likeness of Jesus
- A passion for the lost, as the very heartbeat of God, demonstrated on the cross and imparted by the Holy Spirit
- Establishing, through prayer, an intimate relationship with the God who calls us to ask!
- An aggressive (muscular) Christianity, prepared to go to the people rather than wait for them to come to us. Reaching out to the lost with a holistic gospel concerned about the whole person – body, mind and spirit. A particular passion for the extremities of the human condition, in its most degraded, impoverished and enslaved forms, as a bias shown in Jesus' own ministry
- A pragmatic determination to communicate the gospel in the most appropriate and culturally relevant way that can be found
- A concern for full employment in the salvation war and for the 'priesthood of all believers', including the employment of men and women as equals
- Embracing a sacrificial and dedicated lifestyle as an act of devotion to God and the world
- Searching for excellence in our desire to do everything we do with all our hearts, 'as working for the Lord, not for men' (Colossians 3:23 *NIV*)

Vision and Purpose, Russell Rook, **www.rootsonline.org/vision.asp**, 29 August 2005

[11] Donnelly (1999), pix

Chapter Three

1 Bosch D. *Transforming Mission*, (Orbis Books, New York, 1991), p360
2 Wright C., *The Mission of God* (Nottingham: InterVarsity Press, 2006) quoted in Bosch, p360
3 Larsson J., *Renewal* (London: *The Officer* magazine: 2002), p4
4 Bowen R., *...So I Send You* (Cambridge: The University Press, 1996), p21
5 Quoted in Hunter G., *How to Reach Secular People* (Nashville: Abingdon Press, 1992), p99

Chapter Four

1 Yaxley T., *William and Catherine, The Legacy of the Booths* (Minnesota: Bethany House Publishers, 2003), p15
2 ibid p216
3 Larsson J., *How Your Corps Can Grow* (St Albans: The Campfield Press, 1988), p1
4 Hirsch A., *The Forgotten Ways* (Grand Rapids: Brazos Press, 2006), p110
5 *Imagine*, DVD from The London Institute for Contemporary Christianity
6 Hirsch (2006), pp132-133
7 Robinson M., *The Faith of the Unbeliever* (London : Monarch Books, 1994), p97
8 Atkins M., *Resourcing Renewal* (Peterborough: Inspire, 2007), pp171-174

Chapter Five

1 Begbie H., *The Life of General William Booth, The Founder of The Salvation Army* (London: Macmillan and Company Ltd, 1920), p409
2 Booth W., *Salvation Soldiery* (St Albans: The Campfield Press, no date given), p72
3 Ibid p79
4 Begbie (1920), p408
5 Larsson J., *The Man Perfectly Filled with the Spirit* (St Albans: Campfield Press, 1986)
6 Yuill C., *We Need Saints* taken from the website at: www1.salvationarmy.org.uk/uki/www_uki.nsf/0/EE754D9D83EEE57880256F9600570ED6/$file/Library-WeNeedSaints.pdf
7 Wright C., *The Mission of God* (Nottingham: InterVarsity Press, 2006), p372
8 What can we do in the Army, and indeed the Church, in order to develop and encourage holiness in this area? There are some basic mechanisms that we can consider:

Perhaps the most important thing is to create in our corps a culture of grace, forgiveness and openness, where those who struggle can get support, without condemnation.

We can deliberately develop accountability structures, whether through small groups or, preferably, mentoring relationships. While it is probably true that young men are the most vulnerable in this area, do not discount older men – and women of all ages. Certain leaders in our churches would be well placed to be trained and their awareness could be raised through training and reading.

Teaching on the subject is absolutely essential and, while the Sunday morning sermon will certainly not be a suitable platform, we need to ensure that in small groups we have trained people who can share good teaching and lead discussions in which people can learn and share.

[9] *Salvationist* 5 May 2007
[10] Wright (2006), p374

Chapter Six

[1] Green R., *War on Two Fronts: The Redemptive Theology of William Booth* (Atlanta: The Salvation Army, 1989), p77
[2] Ibid p86
[3] Gamble R., *The Irrelevant Church* (Monarch Publications: Eastbourne, 1991), p98 sourced from J. Moltmann *The Way of Jesus Christ* (SCM: London, 1990)
[4] Ibid p101
[5] *The Seeds of Exclusion* report's executive summary says the report was produced 'in order to understand the indicators in early life which can lead to future problems of social exclusion and to understand the nature, complexity and severity of problems facing people in Salvation Army homeless centres'.
[6] Morisy A., *Journeying Out: A New Approach to Christian Mission* (Continuum, 2004) pp183-184, quoted in Atkins M., *Resourcing Renewal* (Peterborough: Inspire, 2007), p161

Chapter Seven

[1] *Mission-Shaped Church*, (London: Church House Publishing, 2004), p97. A report from the Church of England's Mission and Public Affairs Council.
[2] Hirsch A., *The Forgotten Ways* (Grand Rapids: Brazos Press, 2006)
[3] Meyer F., *Abraham* (London: Morgan and Scott, 1911)
[4] Tillsley B., *The Officer*, Spring 1985

[5] Needham P., *Community in Mission* (St Albans: Campfield Press, 1987), p43
[6] Collins J., *Good to Great* (London: Random House Publishing, 2001), p41
[7] Corps councils and pastoral care councils are not executive, decision-making bodies, but serve the corps officer in an advisory capacity. I would not challenge this, but would simply state that the style with which today's officer leads will need to acknowledge the role and necessity of local leaders owning the vision.
[8] Atkins M., *Resourcing Renewal* (Peterborough: Inspire, 2007), p192
[9] www.methodist.org.uk/downloads/co_871_080408.doc
[10] Mann A., *Can our Church Live?* (USA: Alban Institute, 1999), p26
[11] Ibid

Conclusion

[1] Neilsen, P., *Church on the Move* (Glasgow: Covenanters Press, 2005), p53
[2] Collins, J., *Good to Great* (London: Random House Publishing, 2001)
[3] Booth, W., *The Millennium: The Ultimate Triumph of Salvation Army Principles* (London: *All the World* magazine: 1890), p337

APPENDIX ONE

Health, Healing and Wholeness: The Role of The Salvation Army

Summary

The Cabinet has recommended that a review of mental health, wellbeing and mental health problems be reviewed in Salvation Army social centres, corps and community projects. This work is being underpinned by an extensive and detailed assessment of mental health problems in social centres in which an increasing number of clients have complex needs. These problems are not limited to social centres as corps and community projects provide support to a wide range of vulnerable people.

In reviewing the complex needs of people using Salvation Army social services and attending Salvation Army corps and community programmes, there is an ongoing need to develop an understanding of these needs in order to:

- Consider the role of The Salvation Army in contributing to the mental health and wellbeing of the community

- Provide the most appropriate support for vulnerable people with complex needs

- Assess and reduce risk of Salvation Army staff and volunteers when working with vulnerable people

- Develop partnerships with statutory and non-statutory agencies in the community

- Review the philosophy of care provided by The Salvation Army UKT, within the concept of *Health, Healing and Wholeness*

- Undertake a skills and training needs analysis of staff in Salvation Army social centres and corps and community programmes

- Review existing Salvation Army services with a view to developing same and creating new programmes of support, both specific and generic, for clients with mental health problems

Corps and community consultations

In order to explore the above issues a range of regional/divisional consultations is being undertaken, involving corps/community officers, managers and staff/volunteers.

The International Positional Statement, see below, will hopefully provide a starting point for these conversations.

Dr Adrian Bonner
5 April 2007

Salvation Army International Positional Statement

Health, Healing and Wholeness

Part 3 – Vision and Direction

Vision and Direction Statement

This statement is offered to the entire Army as an affirmation of our ministry of health, healing and wholeness.

Vision

We believe:

1. While God intended health and wholeness for his creation, through sin the world has become sick and is in need of healing and hope (Romans 8:20-21).

2. Because of God's loving nature he has not abandoned the world. Rather, he has taken upon himself our sin, sickness, and suffering in the person of Jesus Christ (Isaiah 53:4-6; 1 Peter 2:24).

3. God is active in all healing. At the deepest level, he has provided for healing and wholeness by spiritual ministries, caring relationships, and the application of scientific insight (Exodus 15:25; Psalm 103:3-5).

4. Jesus healed as a sign of his identity and authority, a manifestation of the Kingdom of God and an expression of God's compassion (Luke 9:37-43; 11:14-20; John 5:36).

103

5. Suffering is a mystery. What we know is that God suffers with us, enables us to bear suffering with courage and trust and, although we cannot fully bear the suffering of another, empowers us to suffer with others in partnership with Christ (2 Corinthians 1:3-7).

6. Wholeness is an expression of holiness. In response to the example and command of Christ, and the presence and prompting of the Spirit, we are called to wholeness in all areas of life, and are given authority to participate in ministries of healing (Matthew 9:35-10:1; Mark 1:41; Romans 8:11; 1 Corinthians 6:12-20).

We therefore affirm:

1. Every Salvationist has the privilege and responsibility of involvement in health, healing and wholeness.

2. Our medical and social programmes make an invaluable contribution. Ministries of health, healing and wholeness are also an integral part of the life and ministry of the corps.

3. God calls his people to utilise their spiritual gifts and dedicated skills in medical and other healing ministries for the enrichment of the Army and the community. These gifts must be exercised under appropriate accountability within the Army.

4. Healing in the Church has many aspects, including acts of loving service to the sick by the laity, healing of the mind and body in response to prayer, and medical and professional services. Medical services are most effective when they are part of a ministry which includes spiritual and social dimensions and involve participation by the community served.

5. Whereas not all will be physically healed through the Church's ministry, the Church is still called to a ministry which includes other dimensions of authentic healing (for example spiritual, emotional, relational, social). Healing includes various degrees of improvement in a person's experience of illness, from slight improvement to dramatic cure.

6. The Army is uniquely positioned to help fulfil the Church's calling to bring a healing ministry to those the society most readily excludes: the poor, neglected and marginalised.

7. We welcome opportunities to collaborate with others in promoting the health of communities. We acknowledge the danger of abdicating our own responsibility, and recognise the need for spiritual discernment in identifying partners.

8. High standards and integrity in our healing ministries must never be compromised.

9. There is a need to encourage gifted persons to enter health ministry fields and it is our responsibility to nurture them.

10. Salvation through Jesus Christ is central to the Army's purpose and provides transforming power in all its ministries. For this reason, evangelism and discipling contribute to health, healing and wholeness.

The Holy Spirit frees and empowers people to seek transformation in all areas of life, resulting in movement towards justice, community change and health.

Direction

Health and wholeness are influenced by many factors, including prayers, evangelism, discipling, compassionate care, social policy, community action and personal choice. Our established services, locations and relationships open many opportunities for ministry.

Love in action is an expression of Salvationist mission. It helps to create an environment in which hope, mutual change and transformation can develop, through God's grace. We demonstrate and experience the Kingdom of God through participation with people in healing.

We enter into partnership through sharing the burdens of people where they are, whether that is in the corps, the institution or the community. Since vision for mission must guide effective action, all Salvationists and others involved in Salvation Army services need opportunity to understand the relationship of their activities to mission.

The basic strategy for integrating our vision with action is design, monitoring and evaluation of implementation, characterised by: sharing of vision, community participation, team building and team work, leadership involvement, transfer of vision, strategies, lessons learned.

A systematic linkage should be developed between needs, goals, existing strengths, activities and desirable outcomes, including reflecting on mission. Tools such as the development planning framework and mission statement formation promote this linkage.

Action and reflection can be strengthened through interactive processes such as technical assistance, consultation and programme-to-programme visits, among others. These processes themselves develop the needed skills, including relationships and trust building, communication, teamwork, documentation, facilitation and community counselling.

Action may change with changing circumstances and needs. However, where there is a vision for mission, direction and impact will be sustained.

Conclusion

We anticipate the need for continuing reflection. We hope for resonance and affirmation from all around the world and present this statement in the hope that it will encourage and guide all Salvationists to recognise and value the heritage, the privilege and the responsibility of the whole Army to participate together in God's ongoing mission of health, healing and wholeness.

APPENDIX TWO

The Seeds of Exclusion

Effective Intervention Research: Community-based Activities Framework

Level One:

- Worship and pastoral care provided to corps members only.

- Very little or no regular community-focused work/support groups provided (eg, breakfast club) by corps.

- No partnerships with external organisations.

- Community-focused work/corps provision (outside worship)* does not adequately reflect needs in local community (eg, deprivation index) or reflect any of the four deliverables**.

Level Two:

- Worship and pastoral care provided to corps members only.

- Some regular community-focused work/support groups provided with church involvement.

- No partnerships with external organisations.

- Community-focused work/church provision (outside worship) does not adequately reflect needs in local community, or more than one of the four deliverables.

Level Three:

- Worship and pastoral care provided to corps members only.

- Some regular community-focused work/support groups provided with church involvement.

- Active partnership with external organisations.

- Community-focused work/church provision (outside worship) does reflect some needs in local community and addresses at least two of the four deliverables.

Level Four:

- Worship and pastoral care provided to corps members only.

- Regular community-focused services/support groups provided with church involvement.

- Active partnerships with external organisations.

- Community-focused work/church provision reflects local community needs well and addresses at least two of the four deliverables.

Level Five:

- Worship and pastoral care provided to corps members and other members of the community.

- Several regular community-focused work/support groups provided with church involvement.

- Several active partnerships with external organisations.

- Mission reflects local community needs well and addresses all four deliverables.

* Worship and pastoral care provided to corps are considered as fundamental and essential elements of effective intervention, community support and inclusivity, within the current research. The current research aims to address not only the spiritual element of community support but also the practical and specialised groups (which can include spirituality) that focus on particular issues in order to increase community development and fit with the four deliverables identified below in previous Salvation Army research.

** The four deliverables are: supporting and sustaining children and families, supporting people in transition, supporting vulnerable people, and speaking out for marginalised people.

APPENDIX THREE – Key Stage One

KEY STAGES – PROCESS DIAGRAM

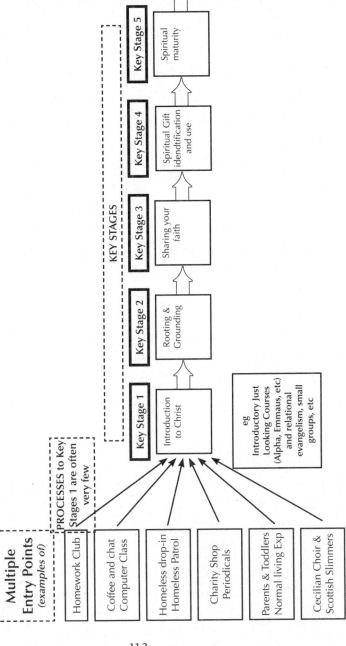

Recommended for further reading

Allen, Roland *Missionary Methods, St Paul's or Ours* (Grand Rapids: Erdmans Printing Company, 1962)

Atkins, Martyn *Resourcing Renewal,* (Peterborough: Inspire, 2007)

Bosch, David *Transforming Mission* (New York: Orbis Books, 1991)

Bowen, Roger *...So I Send You* (Cambridge: The University Press, 1996)

Donnelly, Doris *Retrieving the Charisms for the 21st Century* (Collegeville: The Liturgical Press, 1999)

Gibbs, Eddie *Followed or Pushed?* (Bromley: MARC Europe, 1987)

Hirsch, Alan *The Forgotten Ways* (Grand Rapids: Brazos Press, 2006)

Hunter, George *How to Reach Secular People* (Nashville: Abingdon Press, 1992)

Mann, Alice *Can our Church Live?* (USA: The Alban Institute, 1999, reprinted 2000)

Mission-Shaped Church (London: Church House Publishing, 2004)

Neilsen, Peter *Church on the Move,* (Glasgow: Covenanters Press, 2005)

Newbigin, Lesslie *The Open Secret* (Grand Rapids: William B. Eerdmans Publishing Company, 1978)

Robinson, Martin *The Faith of the Unbeliever* (London: Monarch Books, 1994)

Romano, Antonio *The Charism of the Founders* (Maynooth: St Paul's, 1989)

Sweet, Leonard *Soul Tsunami* (Grand Rapids: Zondervan Publishing House, 1999)

Walker, Andrew *Telling the Story* (London: SPCK, 1996)

Wright, Christopher *The Mission of God* (Nottingham: Inter-Varsity Press, 2006)